A FINANCIAL GUIDE FOR NURSES

Money which represents the prose of
life, and which is hardly spoken of in
parlors without an apology, is, in its
effects and laws, as beautiful as roses.
RALPH WALDO EMERSON
Nominalist and Realist

A FINANCIAL GUIDE FOR NURSES INVESTING IN YOURSELF AND OTHERS

Dorothy J. del Bueno, editor

Blackwell Scientific Publications, Inc.
Boston   Oxford   London   Edinburgh   Melbourne

© Copyright 1981 by Blackwell Scientific Publications, Inc.
52 Beacon Street, Boston, MA 02108 USA

First edition

Library of Congress Cataloguing in Publication Data

Main entry under title:
A financial guide for nurses.
  Bibliography: p. 209
  1. Nursing—Vocational guidance. 2. Nurses—
Finance, Personal. I. del Bueno, Dorothy J.
RT82.F53   332.024'0613   81-10126
ISBN 0-86542-007-6   AACR2

Blackwell Scientific Publications

  Editorial Offices:

  Osney Mead, Oxford OX2 0EL
  8 John Street, London WC1N 2ES
  9 Forrest Road, Edinburgh EH1 2QH
  52 Beacon Street, Boston, MA 02108 USA
  214 Berkeley Street, Carlton, Victoria 3053, Australia

  DISTRIBUTORS:

  Outside North America, except Australia
    Blackwell Scientific Publications Ltd.
    Osney Mead
    Oxford OX2 0EL
    England

  Australia
    Blackwell Scientific Book Distributors
    214 Berkeley Street
    Carlton
    Victoria 3053

Typeset, printed and bound by Haddon Craftsmen, Scranton, PA

Contributing Authors

ANTHONY S. ALFIERI, R.PH.
Sales Representative, Supervisor, District Sales Manager, and Sales Consultant

CHRISTOPHER R. CAMPBELL, PH.D.
Managing Director, Blackwell Scientific Publications, Inc.

GAIL A. CROSSLEY
Nurse Recruitment Consultant, Hospital Corporation of America

DOROTHY J. DEL BUENO, ED.D., R.N.
Assistant Dean, Continuing Education, University of Pennsylvania School of Nursing
Consultant and Lecturer

TANYA I. HANGER, M.S., R.N.
Assistant Director of Nursing, Staffing and Recruitment, New York University Medical Center, University Hospital, N.Y.C.

STEPHEN P. LA BARBERA
Attorney, Certified Public Accountant

MARGO CREIGHTON NEAL, R.N., M.N.
Founder & President, Nurseco, Inc., Pacific Palisades, CA.

J.R. SALISBURY

*The only difference between the rich
and other people is that the rich have
more money.*
MARY COLUM

Preface

Sylvia porter, in her excellent *New Money Book for the '80's,* emphasizes that the American marketplace is an economic jungle that can destroy those who are ignorant of the basic guide for survival. She also notes that most of us are economic illiterates. In my association over the last five years with nurses all over this country and Canada, I find that nurses are interested in, but not well-informed about, economic issues and the uses of money.

For many years nurses were socialized to believe that money was a dirty word. They weren't supposed to be interested in money or concerned with either its acquisition or allocation. Even today, I find some nurses reluctant to discuss salary, fees, or budget. Directors of nursing are often uninformed about finance and accounting practices. Conversely, I have had many requests to advise and counsel nurses on how they might increase their own earning capability and improve their financial situation.

It will take energy, time, and dollars to change your financial situation. All of these are scarce and finite resources. Therefore, you will need to be willing to change how you allocate them. You will need to determine what expenditures or allocations are consumption costs, on which there is no return, or investment costs on which you expect a return. You will need to consider the "lost opportunity cost" associated with each decision. The lost opportunity cost is the possible return or value you lose when you make one choice over another. The lost opportunity cost is never really known since it is hypothetical, but it does need to be considered.

The author and contributors to this book hope it will be helpful in making your financial decisions. The book is intended to be a guide only, not the final answer on any topic. The subjects have been selected on the basis of their interest to the writers and their usefulness to the readers. To learn more about any of these topics, you will want to refer to the Suggested Readings and other texts, articles, and experts. Most of all, don't be afraid to try—experience is still a marvelous teacher, particularly when coupled with knowledge. She or he who hesitates will, in today's economic "jungle," probably end up financially poorer.

Dorothy J. del Bueno
Editor

Certainly there are lots of things in life that money won't buy, but it's very funny—have you ever tried to buy them without money?

OGDEN NASH

Contents

A FINANCIAL GUIDE FOR NURSES

I like my job and am good at it, but
it sure grinds me down sometimes,
and the last thing I need to take
home is a headache.

TV COMMERCIAL FOR ANACIN

1   Finding the Job You Want

Gail A. Crossley

ANY NURSE who's in tune with the times knows that the current job market for professional nurses is booming, with every indication that the demand will continue to increase in the future. The new graduate nurse, the nursing careerist ready for a change, or the nurse seeking re-entry into the job market can pick up the health care help-wanted section in any newspaper across the nation and find the pages peppered with advertisements for a variety of jobs. Not since the post-World War II years have we seen such a growth in the availability of jobs for nurses, both in institutional and non-institutional settings. The job choices are plentiful and diverse, and the nurse who is about to enter practice or make a job change is faced with an awesome number of factors to consider when making an employment decision.

When 17,000 nurses were asked in a *Nursing 78* survey how they felt about their jobs, 79% of the respondents said they were very or moderately satisfied, but the degree of satisfaction varied according to the work setting and the specialty area.[10] Job satisfaction, however, means different things to different people, and the perfect job simply does not exist. The key to the difference between a satisfying nursing career or merely a succession of jobs lies largely within a well-planned job search. That search must have at its

3

foundation realistic expectations and professional career goals based on honest self-assessment.

In caring for patients, nurses are involved in the process of goal setting. Many nurses recognize the value of this in patient care, but never transfer the concept to their own lives. Nursing is such a broad field with so many possible directions that, without carefully set goals, it is possible to drift in the job market for years[9]. Goals will be modified as personal needs change, but career goals should be set early, both on a long-term and a short-term basis.

Self-assessment includes identification of your skills and special interests. In school or in previous jobs, in what area were you most comfortable? Was it in a highly charged, fast-paced ICU, or in a quieter, more predictable setting? What level of autonomy do you seek in your working relationships with patients, peers, and superiors? Where have you gained your experience, and are you considering broadening that experience in a particular specialty? Also, what are your personal needs? What is your geographic preference and would you consider moving or travelling as part of a job? What shift schedules are best suited to your home responsibilities? Do you plan to continue your education?

Self-assessment will provide the basis for the direction of your job search. Without it, you'll waste your time and energy, as well as that of a potential employer! It's a difficult task, and there are no right or wrong answers; what's important is that you make your choices based on your knowledge of who you are as a person.

WHERE THE JOBS ARE

Traditional work settings for registered nurses can be categorized into two main systems: the institutional health care system, and the community health care system. The former includes acute care hospitals and long-term care facilities, while the latter includes public health departments, visiting nurse agencies, private care providers, ambulatory care clinics, and the like. Jobs are more plentiful in the institutional health care system, which employs nearly three-fourths of all active registered nurses.

It has been suggested that the increase in available jobs for nurses can be attributed to three primary reasons. First, the need for professional nurses is increasing as health care is distributed ever more widely, in an increasing variety of settings. In addition, the growing senior population requires more and more nursing service and, finally, as the quality of institutional life changes, more com-plex technologies require hospitals to turn "RN intensive." As greater emphasis is placed on primary care, more nursing jobs within the community health care system will become available. Nonetheless, hospitals and extended-care facilities will continue to be the primary employers of professional registered nurses for the next five to ten years. Short-term, long-term, large, small, urban, rural, Eastern, Western; no matter where you look, the jobs are there.

Jobs Within the Institutional Health Care System

Within the institutional system, a nurse normally begins as a staff or general duty nurse. Staff nurses may specialize in areas of particular interest, such as pediatrics, psychiatry, or obstetrics, or may provide care for patients having specific diseases. They utilize special skills, knowledge, and judgment in providing bedside care and in implementing medical treatment plans prescribed by physi-cians.

An overview of institutional nursing's key areas includes the following[16]:

Medical/Surgical Nursing: Med/surg nurses are skilled in bedside care and trained in every necessary health care procedure, from assisting in diagnostic workups to caring for patients with severe medical problems.

Intensive Care Nursing: Here, critically ill patients receive life-saving and life-sustaining care in a highly specialized and controlled environment. The intensive care nurse is ready at all times to re-spond to even the slightest change in patient status and to function, often independently, in life and death situations.

Obstetric/Gynecologic Nursing: The type of unit in which the ob/gyn nurse works varies according to the institution. For instance, maternity and gynecology units may be separate, in which case there is further specialization: labor and delivery, postpartum, and newborn nursery. Or the obstetrics and gynecology units may be combined, in which case the ob/gyn nurse cares for maternity and gynecology patients and newborns. Besides assisting with hygienic care and performing preoperative and postoperative duties, diag-nostic tests, and treatments, the ob/gyn nurse conducts classes on breast self-examination, feminine hygiene, causes and prevention of vaginal infection, baby care, infant stimulation, breast and bottle feeding, and family planning for maternity patients.

Emergency Room Nursing: ER nurses are well-rounded individuals with a keen knowledge of all nursing areas and disease entities. Emergency room procedures address acute medical, surgical, neurological, and psychiatric emergencies; dead-on-arrival; death in the emergency room; animal bites; rape victims; unconscious patients; abandoned children; obstetrical and gynecological emergencies; poisoning; and overdose.

Pediatric Nursing: In many hospitals, pediatric nurses assume responsibility for the total care of their patients. Parent/child relationships, feeding patterns, growth and development milestones, teaching and discharge needs, and clinical manifestations of illness must be observed, recorded, and reported to whoever needs to know. Clinical procedures which the pediatric nurse usually performs include blood drawing, dressing changes, and spinal taps.

Operating Room Nursing: The OR nurse's first responsibility is to assist physicians with surgical procedures. But today's OR nurses are more than a skilled technicians; they are responsible for planning, implementing, and evaluating care before, during, and after surgery.

Psychiatric Nursing: This nurse's main responsibility is to establish lines of communication with each patient in the psychiatric unit in a sensitive, knowledgeable, clinically sound, and medically objective manner. The psychiatric nurse may work in an intensive inpatient unit, a day treatment service, or an outpatient clinic. Patients might be children ranging in age from several years to adolescence, or adults with specific problems such as drug addiction or alcoholism. The psychiatric nurse is usually a member of a clinical team which also includes a psychiatrist, social worker (or nurse therapist), and other nursing personnel.

I.V. Nurse Therapist: The I.V. nurse therapist is skilled in venipuncture techniques and procedures, and is expertly trained in the use of I.V. solutions, medications, and the various types of I.V. equipment. Since many drugs are often administered intravenously, the I.V. nurse therapist is also trained in drug reactions and appropriate antidotal remedies. Patient rounds are made to ensure that I.V. solutions are being administered efficiently.

Oncologic Nursing: Here, diagnostic procedures and therapeutic regimens are constantly changing as new discoveries in the cancer field are made. The oncology nurse is most often found in a hospital clinic. Daily responsibilities include interviewing patients and assessing their status, discussing treatment plans with physicians, research work, and patient rounds with the medical team, as well as the teaching of both patients and other staff.

Nurse Anesthetist: The certified registered nurse anesthetist (CRNA) provides anesthesia care for a variety of surgical, obstetric, or diagnostic procedures in either a hospital, a private or a group practice. CRNAs have expert knowledge of heart and lung pathophysiology and are well trained in the use of respiratory equipment. Accredited anesthesia programs are available to registered nurses in most states and usually last from 18 to 24 months. A national qualifying examination is necessary, as well as membership in the American Association of Nurse Anesthetists (AANA).

Rehabilitation Nursing: This nurse is responsible for providing rehabilitative therapy to patients with physical limitations caused by illness or injury. The rehabilitation nurse works with children, adolescents, or adults in an outpatient clinic, a vocational rehabilitation center, or in an inpatient setting such as a special rehabilitation hospital or the rehabilitation unit of a general hospital.

Infection Control Nursing: The nurse epidemiologist or infection control nurse is responsible for monitoring an entire hospital for infections, reporting findings to various decision-making groups, and conducting classes, either formal or informal, for hospital personnel on controlling infections among both patients and staff. This nurse has a firm working knowledge of isolation, sterile procedures and techniques, microbiology, immunology, host-defense mechanisms, infectious diseases, statistics, and research methodology. Infection control nurses check constantly to distinguish those infections that developed prior to a patient's admission (community-associated) from those related to hospitalization (nosocomial).

Burn Nursing: The burn nurse must devise individualized plans of total care for patients ranging from pediatric to geriatric. Each such plan must encompass the patient's physical, physiological and psychological needs. Burn nurses are in attendance at the patient's bedside the major portion of the day, where they can directly observe patient status and detect early warnings of complications, initiating proper intervention when necessary. Burn care can be divided into three definable but overlapping periods of treatment: the emergent period, which encompasses the first two to fourteen days postburn, depending on the severity of the injury; the acute period, which begins at the end of the emergent and lasts until all full thickness wounds are covered with autografts; and rehabilitation, when the patient receives rehabilitative therapy which permits the resumption of many normal activities.

The general duty nurse in any of these specialties can advance to the management positions of head nurse, supervisor, assistant or associate director, and director of nursing service. In more than 80% of all institutions these positions are filled through internal promotion. While educational requirements will differ from hospital to hospital, diploma graduates fill many or most of them in more than three-fourths of all hospitals.

The Head Nurse.   The head nurse is usually responsible for the direct and indirect nursing care of patients within an organized unit of a clinical area, such as medicine or surgery, or a specialized unit, such as the ICU or Emergency Room.

The Supervisor of Nursing Service.   The supervisor of nursing service is responsible for nursing care in an area that includes one or more patient units, each of which has a head nurse. Nursing supervisors are also assigned to such areas as the operating room, outpatient department, the recovery room, and special units. Generally, nursing supervisors will be involved in the development and implementation of the philosophy and objectives of the nursing service department, and are usually responsible for planning the kind and amount of patient care needed in their respective areas.

The Director of Nursing and Assistant Directors.   At the top of the nursing service hierarchy is the director of nursing. In many institutions, the director will have one or more assistant directors who may have overall responsibility for entire clinical areas or for certain administrative functions, such as staffing, education, or budgeting. The director of nursing manages and supervises all nursing services concerned with care of patients. In addition to planning the services necessary to achieve the hospital's objectives, the director is also responsible for maintaining the quality of service in accordance with accepted standards. Other functions within the scope of a director's responsibilities may include coordination of services with other departments, development of records, formulation of personnel policies, participation in financial planning for the institution as a whole, and the provision of educational programs. Most contemporary directors of nursing hold masters degrees, either in nursing service administration or nursing education, and have had extensive experience in a supervisory capacity.

Jobs Within the Community Health Care System

Within each community there are many organizations, groups, and individuals offering health care. Some of the more traditional work settings for professional nurses found within the community health care system include the following[18]:

Public Health Nursing: Public (community) health nurses are concerned with preventing illness as well as caring for the ill. They provide nursing care and counsel to individuals and families, in clinics, homes, schools and at work. They also assist in community health education programs involving other nurses, allied health personnel and community groups. Public health nurses are employed primarily in local health departments, schools and voluntary agencies such as visiting nurse associations, but they also work in free clinics, health maintenance organizations, health planning agencies, neighborhood health centers and, increasingly, in private practice. Areas of particular concern in public health nursing include maternal and child health, communicable disease control, chronic illness and rehabilitation, psychiatric care, and nutritional education. The public health nurse visits homes to render nursing service and instruct families in care of patients and maintenance of a healthful environment; gives specialized treatment, following a physician's instructions, to patients afflicted with mental disorders, physical deformities and communicable diseases; assists persons with social and emotional problems to secure aid through community resources, and provides other care and education related to community and individual welfare.

Occupational Health Nursing: To assure that their employees have ready access to basic health protection, many industries and businesses employ occupational health nurses. Sometimes they work alone, or with a physician on call. Often they are public health nurses. In larger organizations they may be part of a health service staff. Following the instructions of a physician, occupational health nurses treat minor injuries and illnesses, arrange for medical care and offer health counseling to employees. They may assist in health examinations and in giving inoculations. They also keep health records of employees and develop programs to prevent or control diseases and accidents among workers. The occupational health nurse works on the premise that the prevention of disease and maintenance of health are as important as the treatment of illness.

Private Care Provicers: Many physicians and some dentists require the services of professional nurses in their office practices. The office nurse helps with physical examinations, in giving immunizations and treatment, in caring for and sterilizing instruments and sometimes does secretarial-receptionist and routine laboratory work. The office nurse may take the patient's basic history, and perform other duties including administering injections, dressing wounds and incisions, interpreting physician's instructions to patients, assisting with emergency and minor surgery, keeping records of vital statistics and other pertinent data of the patient, and maintaining stocks of supplies.

Federal Jobs

One other major category of employment sources for professional registered nurses is the Federal government. Within the U.S. Health Services Administration RNs work in a broad variety of assignments — general and specialized clinical nursing, public health nursing, occupational health nursing, nursing education, nursing consultation, and nursing administration.

Nurses are employed under two systems, the Federal Civil Service and the Commissioned Corps of the U.S. Public Health Service, a uniformed service of the Federal government. Most are employed under the Federal Civil Service system. A baccalaureate degree is required for appointment to the Commissioned Corps, which is comprised largely of professionals in medical and health related fields and serves as a mobile force to combat disease and hazards to human health. Employment opportunities within these two systems can be found in more than 170 Veterans Administration Hospitals, and such U.S. Public Health Service agencies and programs as the Indian Health Service, the Center for Disease Control, and the National Institutes of Health.

Nursing opportunities within the U.S. Armed Forces include

the Army Nurse Corps, the Navy Nurse Corps, and the Air Force
Nurse Corps. Army health facilities range in scope from well-baby
clinics and out-in-the-community public health clinics, to the
highly sophisticated wards of intensive care and the newborn nursery. There are more than 100 Army health care facilities throughout the continental United States, Alaska, and Hawaii. Nurses may
also have the chance to travel and practice clinically in Japan, Ger-
many, Italy, and other countries around the world.

More than 2,500 Navy Nurse Corps officers serve in about
120 hospitals, dispensaries, schools and other Navy facilities within
the United States and at 29 bases in other countries. Navy nurses
provide professional nursing care for the men and women of the
Navy and Marine Corps and their dependents. In addition, they
provide for the teaching, training and supervision of Hospital Corps
personnel.

Air Force hospital facilities range from a small outpatient
clinic to an 1,100-bed teaching hospital, complete with closed-cir-
cuit color television for use in research and training programs.
Specialites open to RNs include coronary care, intensive care, ob/-
gyn, pediatrics, midwifery, mental health, aerospace nursing, flight
nursing, and practitioner-level positions.

RESOURCES FOR JOBS

Job leads for nurses can be found through myriad resources.
Historically, the most successful method of finding a job has been
direct application resulting from personal recommendations and
referrals. Friends, faculty, and family members who can provide
first-hand knowledge about an employer's reputation, working
conditions, philosophies, and other relevant information can be an
invaluable job-finding resource and one that should be utilized
freely.

Advertisements are another excellent resource; and can be
found in a variety of media. Some employers will utilize local radio
and television spots to advertise immediate openings, and will air
them during prime listening or viewing times. Most employers,
however, will advertise in publications of different formats and
frequency of issue. At this writing, new publications aimed at professional registered nurses are hitting the market daily. Listed here
are some of those most widely used for nurse recruitment advertising:

Directories: These are complete reference guides to positions available for registered nurses nationwide in hundreds of hospitals and other agencies. Published annually, they usually contain pertinent articles related to jobseeking, interviewing, resumes, licensing, as well as individual, standardized-format advertisements. These will contain descriptive information about the facility, salary and benefits, working conditions, educational opportunities, and who to contact for more information or to schedule an interview and tour.

Nursing Career Directory
Intermed Communications, Inc.
132 Welsh Road
Horsham, PA 19044

Publication Date:	January
Cost:	Subscribers to *Nursing* are invited to request the Career Directory. To those responding the directory is sent free of charge. Anyone else requesting a copy of the Directory must pay $10.00 in the U.S.A. and $12.00 elsewhere.

Nursing Opportunities
Medical Economics Company
680 Kinderkamack Road
Oradell, NJ 07649

Publication Date:	January
Cost:	$8.95 per copy

Imprint Career Planning Guide
National Student Nurses' Association, Inc.
10 Columbus Circle
New York, NY 10019

Publication Date:	October (Imprint is published five times a year in February, April, September, October and December)
Cost:	Nursing students receive Imprint by joining NSNA. Other interested persons may subscribe at $8 annually in the U.S.

Nursing Job Guide
Prime National Publishing Corp.

470 Boston Post Road
Weston, MA 02193

Publication Date: February

Cost: $15

Journals: More than thirty professional nursing journals currently exist, published either on a monthly, bi-monthly, or quarterly basis. Most address themselves to particular specialties within nursing and most feature recruitment advertising, in display and/or classified form, for positions that are available at the time of publication or in the near future. Usually, a display ad will include a convenient coupon for mail response to the advertiser. Current issues of professional nursing journals and subscription information can be found in community or nursing school libraries.

Newspapers: Newspaper advertising is used by over 90% of all hospital and health care employers to recruit nurses for immediate vacancies. The largest number of ads can usually be found in the Sunday edition. Currently, there are a few nationally circulated newspapers or tabloids that focus primarily on jobs and job-related issues for nurses. These publications also contain recruitment advertising:

Health Care Horizons
P O Box 1069
San Pedro, CA 90733

Frequency: Weekly

Cost: $9 for 52 issues

Nursing Job News
Prime National Publishing Corp
470 Boston Post Road
Weston, MA 02193

Frequency: Monthly

Cost: $8.50 per year

Nursing Careers
P O Box 278
Van Nuys, CA 91408

Frequency: Bi-Monthly

Cost: $18 per year in U.S. and Canada
$9 per year for student nurses

Career days, conventions, and seminars are frequently used recruitment methods and therefore are a good source of job leads. These resources offer the job-seeking nurse the unique opportunity to have direct conversation and face-to-face interaction with the employer's representative or recruiter. This is an excellent time to have questions answered and to collect literature from each representative. Often, facilities are available for on-the-spot interviews. Career days are held at colleges and universities, sponsored usually by the school's placement office or student nurse association. While career days are presented primarily for the benefit of that school's students, very often nurses from the community or neighboring schools are invited to attend as well.

Many state and national associations schedule annual conventions that feature an exhibition of employment representatives. During a well-planned convention, some time is scheduled when no programming conflicts with exhibit hours. This allows ample opportunity for convention attendees to meet and discuss career plans with the exhibitors.

Recently, recruitment resources have included the development of privately sponsored employment conventions for nurses. These are two- to three-day, admission-free functions conducted in major metropolitan centers nationwide. With hours convenient for work and school schedules, these conventions offer nurses and nursing students the opportunity to meet with as many as 125 recruiters from institutions nationwide. As an added bonus, a series of free workshops dealing with job-related issues is usually offered. For more information on dates and locations, contact:

Careers in Nursing Symposiums
National Association of Nurse Recruiters
N. Woodbury Road, Box 56
Pitman, New Jersey 08071

Nursing Career Expositions
Eastern Expositions
P O Box 1285
Fayetteville, North Carolina 28302

Nursing Job Fairs
Prime National Publishing Company
470 Boston Post Road
Weston, Massachusetts 02193

Other resources that may be utilized for job leads are placement offices in educational institutions, announcements of Civil Service examinations, and employment centers operated by the state or local offices of the U.S. Employment Service. If you desire a position in the Army, Air Force or Navy Nurse Corps, or in the Public Health Service of the U.S. Department of Health and Human Services, write directly to the service of choice for information.

Whether you come by your job leads through word of mouth, advertising, employment conventions or otherwise, consider the information in light of your personal career goals — and the employers'. As suggested by Kay Morris and Jim Trygstad in their Entry Into Practice: A Career Entry Guide for Nurses, " . . . just as there is no such thing as the perfect job applicant, there is no such thing as the perfect employer. Also, recruitment advertising, like resumes, is not intended to be brutally honest or bring out the negative. Advertisers will naturally emphasize the positive[14]."

Many terms in these ads and recruitment brochures are subjective by nature. They are not intended to be a contract and should not be interpreted as such. Brochures are intended to capture your interest and motivate you to get more information. Study the information offered. Schedule interviews for firsthand evaluation. Take a tour of the facility whenever possible and discuss any questions you may have with the employment representative. (See the end of this chapter for Questions to Ask.)

There is little need to worry about dishonesty in recruiting. The majority of recruiters today belong to the National Association of Nurse Recruiters, which is a professional organization of hospital nurse recruiters. Each member subscribes to a Code of Ethics that governs both truth in advertising and honesty in recruitment techniques.

THE FINANCIAL REWARDS: SALARIES AND BENEFITS

When *Nursing78* surveyed 17,000 nurses about their jobs, salary was not very high on the list of factors to consider when looking for a new job. Yet, more than 80% of the respondants claimed that salary was important to their overall job satisfaction. Nurses don't enter the profession with the idea of getting rich, but, like everyone else, they do have to eat! Nurses want their salary to reflect what their job is really worth. The good news is that nurses' salaries are moving up, and more nurses feel that they are adequately paid. In 1978, 46% of the nurses surveyed by *Nursing78* thought they were paid a fair salary, compared to 41% who felt they were paid an adequate salary in 1977.

Salaries will differ according to an institution's number of beds, region of the country, and a rural, urban or suburban location. Years of experience will affect a nurse's base hourly rate. The number of years spent in continuous employment with one employer will usually have a greater effect than general experience as a nurse.

In the Spring of 1980, a survey conducted by the National Association of Nurse Recruiters indicated that annual salaries for staff nurses in an institutional work setting ranged from a $13,873 average low to a $17,331 average high. For head nurses, salaries ranged from an average low of $16,350 to an average high of $20,847 and, for supervisors, the range was an average low of $17,742 up to $22,577. Average ranges for directors of nursing went from $23,964 to $29,783. Generally, salaries are slightly higher in the West and Midwest, and in larger hospitals, located either in an urban or suburban area.

Pay differentials are sometimes offered for education or for working in a particular clinical area, such as the Intensive Care Unit. Slightly more than one-third of all institutional employers pay a differential for staff nurses holding BSNs or MSNs, a trend more prevalent in the Northeastern and North Central U.S. Often, however, a baccalaureate or masters degree is a *pre*requisite for a position at a level higher than general duty nurse.

For nurses in institutional health care systems, differential pay for working the evening and nightshifts is almost universal. Evening and night shift differentials may be a straight percentage of hourly base rates or may be offered as a flat dollar amount. The current national average of such increments is 55¢ per hour for evenings and 70¢ per hour for nights.

Salaries for nurses working in jobs within the community health care system will vary with the work setting and job qualifications. The ranges, however, are comparable to those within the institutional health care system.

In the Federal Civil Service system, base pay varies with geographic location. Salary scales are adjusted to be competitive with non-Federal facilities in the area. Depending upon qualifications, current entrance salaries for Civil Service nurses range from $11,243 to $18,101 per year.

Pay and allowances for the Commissioned Corps of the U.S. Public Health Service are the same as for the military services. These are determined by rank and length of service. Entrance salary for corps nurses without dependents is $14,829 per year.

Fringe Benefits

It is not uncommon for workers to overlook the economic and intrinsic value of fringe benefits when seeking a job. However, whether one is self-supporting or is working to supplement other family income, fringe benefits represent real dollars in these inflationary times — some dollars saved and some dollars to spend. Dollars are saved when employers pay the cost of such benefits as health and life insurance; dollars to spend become available with such benefits as paid holiday, vacation, and sick time. In dollars and cents, health care workers are the beneficiaries of benefits equalling 25% to 33% of their incomes. Until recently, workers in industry and the private sector received benefits considered to be superior to those received by health care workers, particularly in hospitals. But now, in an effort to enhance recruitment and retention of employees, particularly RNs, health care employers are providing more attractive benefit packages. Nurses working in federal jobs can expect to receive government benefits, which are usually more liberal than those provided by non-governmental employers. Benefit programs within the government, however, will vary within the different systems and agencies.

Often, benefits are available after a waiting, or probationary, period ranging from three months to one year, and depending upon the particular benefit. Some of the more popular and a few of the newest benefits being offered by employers in the health care system are described here.

Health Insurance: Most plans consist of hospitalization insurance, such as Blue Cross, offering protection against the cost of hospital care, surgery, and other medical services. Usually, this is supplemented by a major medical plan, designed to pay some of the expenses not covered in other plans. Rarely is health insurance not offered, and the majority of employers pay the entire premium for the employee. Often, dependent coverage is available at no or partial cost to the employee. Dental and vision care insurance plans are being offered by increasing numbers of employers, but are not yet the rule.

Life and Disability Insurance: Group life insurance may be a flat dollar amount or will be based on annual salary earned by the employee. Again, this is a universally offered benefit, usually completely paid by the employer. Sometimes, additional amounts of life insurance for the employee and/or dependents can be purchased at low group rates. Disability plans are designed to maintain regular income for employees unable to perform regular duties as a result of illness or injury. This benefit usually offers a percentage of income up to a certain age, most commonly to age 65. Approximately three-fourths of all employers will offer disability insurance and at no cost to the employee.

Retirement Plans: A retirement, or pension plan, is provided by nearly all health care employers. These plans supplement Social Security by paying an income at age of retirement, sometimes as early as age 55. The amount of income is based on earnings at the time of retirement, usually about 45% of that base salary. Tax-sheltered annuities, a type of personal retirement or savings plan, are sometimes available also; your personnel department can advise you as to whether or not your employer qualifies. (Refer to Chapters 12 and 13.)

Professional Liability Insurance: The importance of professional liability insurance for nurses cannot be overstressed. Most nurses are covered at no cost under the insurance policy of the institution that employs them. It's a good idea, however, to seek and obtain written verification of liability coverage from the employer or the employer's insurance agent or insurance company. Individual coverage can be purchased for a reasonable fee, particularly if you are a member of the American Nurses' Association.

Paid Sick Leave: This common benefit provides pay for work time missed due to illness or injury and of a short duration. The most popular sick time offering is a plan whereby paid sick days are accumulated at the rate of one per month, or a total of twelve per year. In an effort to decrease the incident of abuse of paid "sick" days and absenteeism, many employers are lumping together sick time with holiday and vacation time into one annual bank of paid days off. Under this system, which has been more prevalent in industry, employees make no differentiation between days off for sickness, holiday, or vacation and schedule their time off according to the employer's individual policies and procedures.

Leaves of Absence: Depending upon an employer's personnel policies, leaves of absence may be offered for medical, personal, and educational reasons. They are usually without pay and will vary considerably in length of time. Most employers, however, offer a medical leave of absence (which includes maternity) for at least six months.

Vacation and Holidays: The normal amount of paid vacation to expect after one year of employment is ten days. Many agencies allow some vacation time to be taken before a full year's employment, but not usually until after six months of employment. The average number of holidays given is eight per year. Most hospitals pay time-and-one-half to those employees who work on a holiday and straight time to those who get the day off.

Educational Benefits: Tuition reimbursement is a popular benefit, offered by more than 80% of institutional health care employers in the U.S. Usually, this benefit includes a maximum dollar or semester credit limit per year. Most employers offer special orientation or internship programs (mostly for new graduates), and paid time off to attend seminars or continuing education courses. For the nurse re-entering the job market, refresher courses are offered by less than half of all institutional employers. These programs have been costly and have not been very successful for recruitment. Some programs may be found within community colleges or universities.

Additional benefits that are commonly offered to nurses include discounted meals, free or minimal cost parking and credit unions. Some employers also offer uniform allowances, subsidized housing, and relocation and travel expenses.

When considering part-time employment, keep in mind that many of the benefits described here may not be available to employees working twenty or less hours per week. Normally, part-timers can expect to receive pro-rated paid vacation, holiday, and sick time, but the part-time nurse who's looking for paid health insurance, tuition assistance, life insurance and retirement plans will find those benefits offered only by about 20% of employers.

Future salary and benefit patterns within the health care industry will be influenced by the effects of inflation and competition in the labor market. In looking for ways to provide effective economic incentives to their employees, employers will increasingly consider more competitive salary scales, as well as such benefits as dental and vision insurance, more paid time off, and even perquisites such as employer-supplied auto and homeowners' or mortgage insurance.

QUESTIONS TO ASK

At the beginning of this chapter, we discussed the critical importance of setting career goals based on honest self-assessment. To help you find a job that is the most rewarding personally, professionally, and financially consider the following questions in your job search. Based on your personal needs, you'll no doubt want to add other questions of importance to you.

Philosophy of Nursing:

– Do you have a job description and how do the job duties differ from that of other nursing personnel?
– What is the policy if I fail State boards?
– What type of nursing is practiced?
– What is the organizational structure in the Nursing Department?

Education:

– What are the educational benefits?
– How regular are inservice programs and are they offered on all shifts?
– Does the employer pay for seminars, workshops, and conventions?
– Explain the length and content of orientation.

Advancement:

– How long is the probationary period?
– How frequently is my performance evaluated and by whom?
– What are the requirements for management positions?
– Explain the transfer policy.

Salary and Benefits:

– What is the starting salary and what differentials are offered?
– How are time schedules prepared and what are the scheduling requirements?
– Who pays for health benefits for me and my family?
– Explain other benefits and effective dates.

Finally, when looking for the job you want, you'll want to consider what it is that employers are looking for when they recruit and hire nurses, aside from specific qualifications such as experience and education. Truly, job opportunities for nurses abound across the nation, but that fact does not guarantee your getting the job **you** want! In addition to sound technical and communications skills, employers will look for other qualities like flexibility, common sense, initiative, stability, sound judgment, sensitivity, and good interpersonal skills.

Finding the job you want involves some gambling on your part, as well as the employer's. There are no guarantees for success. But, with a sound knowledge of yourself and your goals, and a carefully planned and implemented job search, the odds are in your favor for a satisfying career as a professional nurse.

Work keeps us from three great evils:
boredom, vice and need.

VOLTAIRE

2 Getting the Job You Want

Tanya I. Hanger

INTRODUCTION

JOB HUNTING in the 80's presents an interesting predicament for nurses: too many options. Not too long ago there was a very different situation: too few positions for too many applicants. That situation generated a lot of anxiety in new graduates who feared they had no chance of getting the job they wanted. Because of the fear of not getting the desired job, individuals might apply to fifteen or more institutions or settle for less than they would have liked, seeking safety and security in a guaranteed place. Experienced nurses were able to find work, but had to look a little longer. They were not always assured of getting their first choice of service either.

Now, however, the circumstances are just the reverse. Nurses have more job opportunities than they are interested in. What has caused this change in the job market? First, the hospital environment has changed, with more acutely ill patients as well as patients who stay shorter periods of time. There are also many more patients in extended care facilities and in home care situations. Second, there are more intensive care patients, requiring a higher nurse-to-patient ratio. Third, the population is aging, thus increasing the number of people with illness. Fourth, enrollments in nursing programs are down as a result of a decrease in population and an increase in career choices for women, who comprise 98% of the nursing profession.

Knowing there are many employers who want you can make your job search exciting, but don't be lulled into complacency. Getting the right position will involve hard work. There are right positions for nearly everyone. In order for you to be satisfied with your ultimate choice, it is important that you take time to go through the following five steps.

(1)   Assess your job priorities.
(2)   Present yourself positively through your resume.
(3)   Follow job leads.
(4)   Learn to play the Interview Game.
(5)   Review your priorities using trade-offs, and make your decision.

These steps may take time but will help move you through all of the components of a decision-making process, from assessment to evaluation. If you go through each of these steps thoughtfully, you will find the position that's right for you.

ASSESSING YOUR JOB PRIORITIES

There aren't many, perhaps not any, **perfect** jobs. But if there were, this is how they would be described based upon interviews with hundreds of nurses. The components of a perfect job would include: doing what you want to do in a pleasing physical environment; getting the recognition you deserve; having the opportunity to learn and grow; working the hours you prefer for a fair salary; and working with people you find compatible. Sounds perfect, doesn't it?

Rank each of these components in level of importance to you. For example, does salary rate higher than recognition? Would a city environment make all other factors unimportant? To these factors add any others personally important; and you have completed the first step in the decision making process.

Don't be hasty. This priority list will be your most important tool for getting a job that is satisfying, rewarding, and the right one for you. Remember that your written priority list may be different from your "real" priority list. Imagine your priority list looks like the following.

(1)   Shift, or hours worked.
(2)   Pay.

(3) Location.
(4) Learning opportunity.
(5) Choice of service.
(6) Opportunity for advancement.
(7) Recognition.
(8) Good working relationships.

Think back to any job you have left. If your reasons for leaving were a breakdown in communication between you and your fellow employees or supervisor, or little recognition for what you did, and little, if any, learning opportunities, then you should reorder your priority list.

Think about what you said to your employer when you left. The reasons most commonly given to employers for leaving are: "The hours don't fit my life style; the pay is too low; the traveling time is too long; I'm going to school; I'm moving." However, when you told your friends you were leaving your job, what did you say to *them?* Probably something like this: "I'm tired of working so hard when nobody cares or listens to me," or, "I can't stand my supervisor — she only tells me when I do something wrong."

Go back to your priority list again. If you look closely, you may see that what you have written as your last two choices are really the first two reasons for your leaving your previous job. Rearrange your list.

DEVELOPING A RESUME

Having assessed your priorities you have a clear picture of the package that is uniquely you. How can you sell that package to a prospective employer?

Your resume, or curriculum vitae, is often your introduction and your first selling tool. The resume is a brief account of your education and employment background. Include your name, address, and telephone number. Give a short statement of your career goals or objectives, your work background, and your educational qualifications. A resume should be one to two pages in length and should always be sent with a brief, typed original cover letter indicating your interest in and qualifications for the position you are seeking. There are many good resources for format and style on writing resumes or curricula vitae in your local library.

Writing an effective resume is a thoughtful and time-consuming task. Consider the employer's time and situation. Most resumes are not very effective because they fail to meet one or more of the following criteria:

(1) *Brevity:*   Two pages maximum for experienced practitioners, one page for recent graduates. When an interviewer has two telephone calls waiting, several people in the reception room, and ten resumes on her desk, she is unlikely to consider any that are four pages long. You can always provide more detail on request.

(2) *Appearance:*   An attractive, clear, format that is easy to read makes the interviewer's job much easier. Prepare an original or a very clean copy for each application; a resume which is a fifth carbon copy or a poor photocopy creates the impression that you attach little importance to the job or yourself.

(3) *Individuality:*   Statements that reflect your interest and experience in specialty areas or identify how you are different from the other applicants with similar qualifications will increase your chances of getting the job or at least of having a successful interview.

(4) *Cover letter:*   A typed cover letter that indicates which specific job you are interested in and qualified for. (Remember, an interviewer may have several different jobs to fill.)

Do not include your age, marital status, or country of origin in the resume. These can be prejudicing statements that prevent you from being contacted for an interview. Also, be careful about stating flat salary requirements. A range or negotiable salary is better.

Resumes should be typed. If you do not type, there are agencies that specialize in doing so. If you use a resume service, you will probably get an attractive format, but you still have to work on providing effective data and content.

If you find you have more to say than will fit into two pages, don't say it! Indicate that more information is available on request.

Statements about your work responsibility should be clear and concise, not more than two to three sentences. If you are applying for the position of clinical supervisor and you have a strong teaching background, emphasize whatever leadership experience you have. If you are applying for an inservice job, emphasize that experience. In other words, tailor your resume to the position.

JOB LEADS

How to find the kind of job you want is discussed in the preceding chapter. For entry-level positions, look in journals such as *The American Journal of Nursing, RN, Nursing, Nurse Educator,* and newspapers. Career days and job fairs are also primary means of learning about job opportunities.

Frequently, good jobs are heard of by word of mouth or through search firms. The old saying, "It's not what you know, it's who you know" is very true. Knowing the right person is probably the most important method used to obtain the right job.

Richard Nelson Bolles, author of *What Color Is Your Parachute?,* spends a great deal of time discussing how to conduct a job search by establishing job contracts[5]. The need for contacts is one good reason to join and attend meetings of professional organizations as well as school alumni meetings. Refer to Bolles' book for more specific help in how to establish job contacts if you do not have them already.

What about agencies or search firms? Nurses looking for staff nurse positions do not need to use agencies because of the nation wide availability of openings. Nurses who are looking for top jobs, especially in management, frequently use search firms because of their national scope. This is especially true of nurses who want to or are willing to relocate.

Whether you use an agency, make contacts at a conference, or respond to a magazine or newspaper ad, you hope ultimately to meet with an actual employer. This contact usually involves making an application. If there is a form to complete, you should receive it within two weeks of a written or phoned request. If you do not receive it, call. After mailing the completed application, you should hear from the employer within two weeks. Several employers out-line the steps to take in their brochure material. Again, if you do not hear, call.

When you are called for an interview, determine what exact process you are to follow. Some places may want you to come back two or three times. Advise them if you are from out of town and have time constraints. Also determine who will pay for any travel expenses. Sometimes multiple appointments can all be scheduled in one day.

THE INTERVIEW GAME

Now that you have listed your job priorities, composed your resume, and obtained some leads resulting in appointments, you are ready to play the "Interview Game."

Once you have an appointment, these five pointers will help you get the interview off to a good start:

First, be on time! You may have to wait, but if you keep **them** waiting you might set the stage for a negative interview. Therefore, allow plenty of time for travel, parking, and finding the right office.

Second, choose carefully what you wear. Probably the best advice is to wear something you feel good in, but in any case keep it conservative. For example, a suit or skirt and jacket outfit would be better than designer jeans. If you believe that what you wear doesn't matter, listen to this story recently overhead on the subway. Two people (apparently from the same office) were discussing a job applicant: "Did you see what that guy had on? A pair of plaid pants. His jacket didn't match and his tie was dirty. Besides, he looked like . . . and you know how awful he was. I sure don't want him for that job." The applicant never even gave himself a chance to be considered for the job.

Third, be polite no matter how much you may disagree with the person interviewing you. Don't argue; it gets you nowhere, and you will be considered abrasive. That doesn't mean that you can't state your opinion and even disagree. The trick is to get your point-of-view across without being labeled as too aggressive. A good approach is to acknowledge the interviewer's points first and than share your own opinions.

Fourth, don't schedule interviews too close together. When you have appointments with different employers at 9:30AM, 11:30AM and 2PM, you are taking a big risk that you will either miss your 11:30AM appointment, or be late. If that happens, your 11:30AM interview will be stressful, and your 2PM appointment could be a disaster.

Fifth, do your homework ahead of time. Think through what it is you want to accomplish during each interview. If you are nervous, and most people are in this situation, you may not be able to think of anything to say if you are not properly prepared. That makes it very difficult for the interviewer to get any feeling about who you are as a person. The more convincing you are with the interviewer the greater possibility you have for getting the job. When you do get nervous, remind yourself why you are right for this position. This may give you the confidence you need.

Let's assume that you have followed all of these guidelines and are now ready for the actual interview. It is the interviewer's responsibility to begin the conversation, often by reviewing the application. Be prepared to answer questions about how long it took to get to the interview, what mode of travel you used, and how you would travel when working, particularly if off hours are part of the job. The interviewer will probably ask about your license or permit, and review your work history. Tell the interviewer what position you are interested in and what shift preferences or time limitations you have. Most interviewers try to set a tone that will help the applicant relax as much as possible. Some interviewers will be casual, others will be formal, but all expect the candidate to be prepared and to try to make a favorable impression.

New graduates should be prepared to explain how much and what kind of clinical experience they've had. The experienced nurse should be prepared to answer what she did and didn't like in her previous work, and why she left the previous position.

If you are a new graduate applying for a job in a specialty unit, in intensive care or in public health, you need to be able to support your request for such a position rather than in a general medical or surgical unit. Also, if you had difficulty in certain school subjects, reflected by poor grades on a school transcript, you may be asked for an explanation.

Experienced nurses may be asked about attendance on previous jobs. Prolonged absences or gaps in employment probably will be explored. Be prepared to discuss how you deal with stress and whether or not you believe you can profit from constructive criticism.

Know your strong and weak points and be able to describe them, preferably with examples. Be prepared for questions that explore your problem-solving ability. Know what your career plan is and if further education is a part of that plan. Consider what kind of a time commitment you are prepared to give if you are selected for a position. A prospective employer will want to know this.

You should not be asked personal questions regarding your marital status, whether or not you have children, and any other question dealing with your personal life that will not directly affect your work performance.

An interview is a two-way street, and knowing what questions to ask can be as important as the answers you give. Issues to explore in the interview include:

(1) *Housing.*   Many urban hospitals have apartments or dormitory space for nurses. If you need and are interested in this kind of housing, find out the location as well as the cost and whether or not there is a waiting list. If you intend to buy or rent your own housing ask about the real estate situation in the area. (Also refer to the advice in Chapter 10 on buying or renting.)

(2) *Shifts — Permanent or Rotation.*   More and more nurses seek a straight day position. If you are required to work evenings or nights, you need to know the length of that commitment and what, if any, is the salary differential. If the day shift rotates to cover other shifts, you need to ask how this is done and how often it occurs. An exact answer to this question is impossible, but you can get a rough idea.

(3) *Weekends/Days Off.*   Few nurses enjoy working weekends, and every other weekend off is becoming more and more common. Some agencies have ten or twelve hour shifts, four-day work weeks, seven days on/seven days off schedules, or position sharing. All of these staffing options are attempts to attract nurses and to keep them in the work environment. Know what type of schedule best suits you, and ask if it is a possibility. If you have professional or personal commitments that require specific days off, inform the interviewer of this need.

(4) *Work Assignment.*   In general, nurses like to work with specific kinds of patients. Nurses do not like to "float" because they feel responsible for a group of unknown patients with problems for which they do not have the required clinical experience. Therefore, know whether you will have to cover for other nurses' patient loads or districts during vacation or illness periods.

(5) *Patient-nurse Ratio.*   Numbers are not always indicative of time needed to care for a patient load. You need to know the acuity of illness, the number of nurses available, and also whether or not there is a supervisor, ancillary personnel, or clerical support services.

(6) *Acuity Level.*   Find out something about the kind of patients and their needs for nursing care. Even the label given to a unit may be misleading. All medical patients are not alike nor are all surgical patients. You can't simply go by the label.

(7) *Delivery of Care.*   There may be a discrepancy between the stated method for providing nursing care and how it is actually organized. If you are told that the agency practices primary or team

nursing, explore exactly what that means. In an interview, you may not have the benefit of observation, so be sure to define terms.

(8) *Orientation.*   All new positions require some type of orientation. How long orientation lasts is usually perceived differently by the persons receiving and giving it; the duration being anything from several days to several months. Whatever the agency states as its orientation policy, you will receive on-the-job training, to a greater or lesser degree. You will be expected to learn agency procedures and tasks with or without any formal feedback from an instructor or preceptor. Find out about the feedback system. You will probably carry a full workload before you know how to deal with all the possible problems. You may or may not have a resource person available on request. Discuss the role of that person if possible. In the interview, find out if there is any formal classroom instruction and for how long. Also discuss on-the-job supervision. How long will this be available? Who will provide this supervision?

For both the new graduate and the experienced nurse, the time following orientation is of crucial importance. Beginners often feel that they cannot cope and that there is no one who will help. Experienced nurses often feel as though the staff does not trust them. Experienced people sometimes alienate others by saying "At Hometown General, we did it this way." Find out as much as possible during the interview about the people with whom you'll be working in order to avoid getting off on the wrong foot.

(9) *Salary and Fringe Benefits.*   Salaries and fringe benefits are fairly uniform within a given geographical area. Nearly all health-related agencies have listings of their benefits in a brochure or benefit sheet. If possible, get this information before the interview so you can discuss any specific questions. Common benefits are vacation, holiday time, personal days, sick time, hospitalization insurance, disability insurance, life insurance, malpractice insurance, pension, tuition reimbursement, and leaves of absence.

In agencies with collective bargaining contracts, salary is set with possible additions for education and/or experience. Experience differentials are usually paid for five-years-and-over experience. That means that a nurse with five years' experience and a nurse with eight years' experience could start at the same salary.

Education differentials may be paid to nurses who have a BSN or a Masters in Nursing. Nearly all agencies pay differentials to staff nurses working permanent evening or night hours. There may also be differentials for rotating shifts. While there are general geographical rates, it pays to check out individual practices since they vary as much as $1,000 per year.

It is generally accepted that applicants do not discuss benefits first. At the end of the interview, especially if you are interested in the position, it is appropriate to ask about salary if the interviewer has not already addressed this subject. Then, if you do not know the other benefits, ask for a quick rundown.

(10) *Unions, Bargaining Agents, Professional Organizations.* Although seldom discussed during interviews, unions can have a great bearing on your overall job satisfaction. In order to discuss unions intelligently, you should have some basic understanding of them.

Unions, bargaining agents and professional organizations are terms used when nurses indicate that they are represented by a third party. In many instances, the third party is the economic security branch of the State Nurses' Association. That means that nurses in California who have this type of representation will refer to it as the California State Nurses' Association (CSNA); Ohio nurses as the Ohio State Nurses' Association (OSNA); and so on. There may, of course, be other types of third party representation. The staff tend to call their state organization their bargaining agent. Management, on the other hand, tend to call this type of organization a union.

Contract hospitals, those which have bargaining agents for employees, must negotiate a contract between the employees and management at determined intervals. The typical time is two years. The contract establishes terms for both the employees and management. Some things are very clear. For example, salary is set with agreed-upon intervals, usually annual, for increases. A contract also covers whether or not a differential is paid for education, shift, and experience. It establishes a probationary period, who gets laid off in periods of economic cutback, and the grievance procedure. It also describes who is and who is not to be included in the union. Contracts reflect the values and the needs of the people who negotiate them. The major advantages of contracts are recognition for seniority, provision of a group for representation, and consistency in specific contractual areas.

What you need to know is the presence or absence of a collective bargaining unit and the major contractual commitments. A historical perspective of when and why the agency became unionized is helpful, particularly if you are seeking a supervisory position. However, the circumstances that initiated unionization may no longer be relevant, so keep this information in perspective. Also if recognition and working relationships are important to you, find out if strife exists because of the presence of a union.

(11) *Job Descriptions and Evaluation Practices.* Almost every agency has formal job or position descriptions. These may be very specific or very general. The job description gives some information about the responsibilities and duties of the employee, but they may or may not reflect reality in detail. You probably won't know this until you are in the actual job. However, the description will give you a sense of the complexity, difficulty, and variability of the position. Does the description sound reasonable and relevant? Does it describe the kinds of responsibilities you are able or willing to assume? Although the agency may not wish to give you a copy of the job description, they should be willing to let you review it. If not, ask why. What's the big secret? Job descriptions tend to be vague for high level positions. This is reasonable since it may be difficult to describe the exact functions of administrative positions. However, you should know what goals or objectives you will be expected to accomplish.

Most organizations also have some kind of evaluation process. Ask how often or under what circumstances you will be evaluated. Who will do your evaluation: self, peers, supervisors, or some combination? Are salary, benefits, or other rewards tied to evaluation results? Is there a specific evaluation tool? If so, is it based on job expectations or on personality characteristics? There are not necessarily right answers to any of these questions. However, the answers given should give you additional information about the organization and its values.

(12) *Recognition and Interpersonal Relations.* How can you know ahead of time whether or not you will receive recognition for what you do? What are the working relationships among people and departments? You can't find out exact answers to these questions, but there are several things you can do that will minimize uncertainty. Speak to at least two people in positions similar to the one you are seeking. Ask them how they like their jobs. Ask them if staff get along, and if there is any positive feedback from supervisors, administration or other professionals. It is difficult to do this when visiting the department with an interviewer or another employee. However, some agencies will provide you with a time when you can talk to staff alone. (Doing this is usually a plus indicator for the organization.)

If it is not possible to talk with people in the work area, try to talk with people in the cafeteria. Of course, if you only talk to one person, you are probably going to get a biased account, so try to hear several points of view. Also, ask people why they chose to work in the organization and what they would change in the work situation if given the opportunity.

Besides asking staff these questions, you need to be alert when visiting the work area. Remember that not only is your tour guide evaluating you, you are also evaluating her or him. Observe how staff relate to the person you are with. Is there an air of friendliness, of respect, or of resentment? When observing the work area, it is like seeing one piece of a picture. Perhaps it's a day when more or less than usual is happening. There may be a many or few staff visible. The number can be indicative of staffing inconsistencies or that everyone is busy with patients. Seeing the work area on one occasion is only an indicator of the actual situation, but it can be helpful, especially in guiding you in the questions you ask.

If you are applying for a management or education position it might be helpful to attend a management meeting, a committee meeting, or an educational activity. Again, one example is a meager sample.

While these are not foolproof methods for evaluating staff relationships, they are better than none. Some applicants take an unaccompanied walk through the agency to evaluate the atmosphere. Whatever your method, think about it ahead of time and *know* what you are looking for.

Special Considerations

Most of the issues mentioned so far relate to any type of position. The person who is looking for advanced job placement will have additional interview concerns.

(1) *The reason for the vacancy.*   Why didn't this job go to someone already in the organization? It is often true that agencies promote from within. Therefore, it is a good idea to try to find out why no one within the organization got the job you seek. Why did the person or persons in the job previously leave the position? What is the turnover rate in this position? If you can find out the real story, you may still want to be considered for the job; or you may want to withdraw your application.

(2) *Organization Philosophy.*   Find out something about the organization's philosophy and leadership/management style. Who

participates in decision making? Do orders come down from the top to be implemented by everyone else? You can usually find out the answer to this question by listening. Most of us give away answers if we talk long enough. That's a good reason for seeing several people in the organization hierarchy. Someone ultimately will give you the kind of information you seek.

Is the department philosophy based on a single theory or conceptual framework? Some institutions may not have a clearly defined answer. You need to know, however, if the general philosophy is compatible with your values or is acceptable to you. For example, if you are committed to concepts of primary nursing and are told that there are more licensed practical nurses and aides than registered nurses, you will either have to modify your concept of nursing or hope to change the philosophy in order to accept a position in that institution comfortably.

The same quandary applies to educational philosophy or management philosophy if you are seeking a job in education or management. If you are a traditionalist, a teaching job in a nontraditional or competency-based institution would require a shift in values — yours or theirs.

(3) *Status.*   Where does the position fit in the table of organization or organization chart? Who reports to whom? How many positions are there on the administrative, professional and support levels? While some organizations will not give out a copy of their table of organization they will usually give you an oral account. The formal organizational structure may not be the same as the informal structure. How will you know this? Again, this can sometimes be learned by careful listening and by talking with various people within the organization. How do various departments relate to one another? Who chairs important committees? Who goes to which meetings?

(4) *Authority.*   How much authority will you have? If you are seeking a staff position such as an instructor or clinical specialist, you will not have any line authority and, therefore, little formal power. You will be expected to explain, teach and subscribe to the philosophy and values of the organization, but will have no authority to hold people consistently responsible for compliance. This is the crux of staff positions, responsibility without positional authority, and must be considered if you have a strong need for authority and formal power.

If you are seeking a line position, such as a supervisor, chairman, or administrator, then you will certainly have power in the formal sense. However, both managers and administrators frequently perceive themselves as having little if any real power because it is so clearly delimited. It goes so far, but no farther. When applying for a management position, it is a good idea to find out how that position is viewed by both administration and staff.

If you do your homework, and fully utilize interview opportunities, you should accomplish several things. You'll decide what type of power structure best suits you, investigate the formal and informal realms of power within the institution, and see where the position you are applying for fits within this structure. Then, you can determine whether a position is not for you or just right for you, or that the position is risky, but you still want to give it a try.

(5) *Additional Expectations.*   Many faculty and administrative positions have responsibilities other than the specific job requirements. Some examples are: social activities such as hosting visiting dignitaries or attending organization functions; community activities, such as giving educational programs to lay groups, or participating in health fairs, mayor's committees, or Board of Health sub-committees; public relations, such as speaking at conventions, participating in recruitment drives, or giving press conferences. Publishing and doing research may be included in the position description or may be an unstated but actual expectation. There may also be unwritten but clear expectations about what you can't do while in the job such as political action, freelance consultation, or moon-lighting. Don't assume that you know what these additional expectations or no-no's are. In fairness to you and your perspective employer, find out.

(6) *Salaries, Benefits and Promotion.*   Salary and benefits may be more negotiable for higher level positions. Be sure to discuss what the ranges and options are for the position. What promotional opportunities are available and how will you qualify? Do you need advanced education in addition to effective work performance? How often do these opportunities become available? Is there a search committee to fill the job? Historically, has the organization gone outside to fill its top jobs? Again, answers to these questions will give you a better sense of the organization and its practices.

(7) *Multiple Interviews.*   Some positions require that candidates go through interviews with search committees or with many different individuals. These multiple interview situations can be anxiety-producing and time-consuming. In the best circumstances,

you will know who you are going to meet with and what they will ask you, but these best circumstances are rare. Many search committees and individuals are inexperienced in the interviewing process and do not use a systematic format. So, be prepared for anything. Know your assets and limitations. Know why you want the position, your career goals and what you have to offer that is unique and relevant. Get as much information as possible before the interviews about the organization, its mission, its financial status, its personnel practices, and management style. While both you and the organization have a right to withhold certain information, it will be helpful if all parties are as candid as possible.

Don't be afraid to say you don't know how to answer a question or that you would need to give it some thought. No answer is better than a stupid answer.

Interview Follow-up

Whatever your reaction to the interview, and whatever type of position you seek, you should know what follow-up is expected. If this is not clear to you, ask. The interviewer or committee may need time to check references, to interview other applicants or to consult with other people in the organization. Know whether you are expected to initiate a follow-up or give an answer in a specific time. Always be sure to clarify whether or not you want your current or past employers notified of the fact that you are seeking employment to avoid embarassing situations for yourself and others.

After a series of interviews you may have a choice of job offers. If you are asked to make a commitment during an interview, request time to decide, even if you are sure you want the job. This is nearly always possible. If you are not asked to make a commitment at the interview, clarify when you should expect an offer or to make a commitment. Should you leave the interview without knowing the expected follow-up, call and find out.

MAKING TRADE-OFFS AND A FINAL DECISION

Your final decision will be affected by your initial priority list. You may have to choose a less-than-ideal position because of these pre-established priorities. You may feel forced to accept a job because of these priorities, but explore all means of making the situation more acceptable. For most of us, any job we take will require some trade-offs. No job is perfect. Re-examine your priorities and decide which you are willing to give up in order to get what you want. Do this carefully, and you will lessen the chance of future resentment.

Having options helps us feel better about what we ultimately choose to do. Even if you are not limited by your personal situation you still have choices, since all jobs have certain drawbacks. Trade off the positives and negatives in relation to your own personal priorities. Using the original sample priority list, what trade-offs are there?

(1) *Shift.*   I have to float, but I have a straight day job.

(2) *Pay/Benefits.*   They don't practice primary nursing, but the pay is terrific. Or, I don't agree with the philosophy, but I get summers off.

(3) *Location.*   It only takes me five minutes to get to work, but I can't stand my boss. Or, I travel two hours a day to and from work, but I have great flexibility and freedom in the job.

(4) *Learning.*   People really take time to teach you here, but it takes a long time to advance. Or, orientation was really too short, but the pay and location couldn't be better.

(5) *Service.*   Rotation is terrible, but I got my first choice of service. Or, patients with chronic disease are not my favorite, but I'm learning so much I want to stay.

(6) *Advancement.*   Half the faculty are giving me a very hard time, but I enjoy the challenge of being course chairman. Or, I decided to accept less salary because there is great opportunity for rapid advancement.

(7) *Recognition.*   The staff really support me, even though the physicians don't want to acknowledge my position. Or, I really enjoy the challenge even though I never get any positive feedback.

(8) *Good working relationships.*   The place has problems, but my group work together and support one another. Or, the tuition benefits are worth whatever I lack in friends on the job.

The preceeding tend to be either/or statements covering a range of compromises. Ideally, you want your priority list to have as few negative statements as possible.

SUMMARY

The component steps in a job search are assessment, planning, action, and evaluation. In your search, assessment of both yourself and the situation is probably the most important initial step. Evaluation, however, is the most difficult step. Begin now to practice careful evaluation of options, choices, and variables and you will make better career choices. It is the combination of poor initial assessment and evaluation of the employment process that generally initiates the phenomenon called "job hopping."

Re-evaluate your priority list before you look for a job. Use this revision to construct your resume carefully and evaluate which job leads to follow. Even the interview is a two-way process of evaluation. Evaluate your decision options in relation to your priority list using a system of trade-offs. Finally, follow your instincts. The element of "gut feelings" should not be underestimated. If you have followed these suggested steps you will have an excellent chance of making an intelligent professional choice, and getting the job you want.

ADDENDUM

The preceding two chapters described where the traditional nursing jobs can be found and how to get them. The marvelous thing about nursing however is the almost unlimited additional opportunities for employment. The skills and knowledge learned in the practice of nursing can be used in a great variety of ways.

First consider other types of nursing positions. Nurses practice in school systems, in Family Planning Clinics, in blood banks, in the American Red Cross, in industry, banks, department stores, camps, and on cruise ships. Some nurses have positions in organ transplant services, on research teams, on nutritional support teams, and as rehabilitation specialists. There are nurses who serve as consultants to marketing departments for health related services, publishers of materials for health professionals, instructional media producers, health departments or government agencies. There are nurses who are professional full-time writers, editors, publishers, executive directors of professional organizations, and lobbyists. *The American Journal of Nursing* in a January 1981 article[3] interviewed nurses in different capacities in the Federal Government, including an advisor to the Senate Finance Committee and a legislative aide.

Chapters 3, 4, 5 and 6 address opportunities for nurses as sales professionals, as business owners, as consultants and lecturers. Although these are not the kind of positions for which nurses are traditionally educated and prepared they are meaningful options. It will become obvious to you that to be successful in one of these untraditional roles you will need to acquire new skills and knowledge and redirect some present abilities. Some of you may even feel guilty at the thought of leaving the practice of patient care. Nursing is a process used to help individuals identify, solve and cope with problems. If this is what you like to do then any of these other options allow you to do just that, only in a different setting, under different circumstances, or in a different context.

If you like what you are doing now and where you're doing it, fine. Stay with it. But, if you would like to do something else there are opportunities — you only need to seek them out and prepare for them. If the opportunity you are looking for doesn't currently exist, sell someone on your special skills, knowledge, and contribution. Don't wait for it to come along; make it happen!

II OTHER OPPORTUNITIES

3 So You Want to be a Consultant

Dorothy J. del Bueno

A CONSULTANT HAS been defined as someone who carries a briefcase and is twenty-five miles from home — or someone who blows in, blows off, and blows out. In reality, a consultant generally is someone who, on request, shares an expert knowledge or skill with a consultee, or helps the consultee achieve specific objectives. A consultant provides a service to the consultee. This service may be free or for a fee. A common characteristic of most consultant-consultee relationships is that it is voluntary. The consultee initiates both the request and the relationship. Anyone considering a consultative role needs to be aware of the important implications of this voluntary element. Since the client or consultee initiates the relationship, the consultant will, in some way, need to be known as credible, available, and capable of providing the desired service. The first task of the consultant, therefore, is to establish credibility and capability.

ESTABLISHING CREDIBILITY AND CAPABILITY

Rule number one for consultants — *Know what you can do and what you can't.* Most consultants have a few areas of expert knowledge or skill. No one can be a consultant on everything. Having an opinion or some experience is not the same as being an expert. The area in which you choose to be a consultant should be both theoretical and practical. Theoretical means being well versed in the content related to the subject. Content and theory might be focused on clinical practice such as cardio-vascular nursing, rehabilitation or high risk pregnancy. Content could also be focused on functional subjects such as performance appraisal, quality assurance, or staff development programming. Content changes constantly, so you must continuously update what is current through education, books, journals, and research studies. A consultant is not expected to have all the answers, but should be familiar with most of what is known in the chosen area of consultation. If the consultee knows more than the consultant, there is little need for the service.

Be practical. This means that you should have experience using the knowledge or skill in a variety of contexts and under a variety of circumstances both similar to and different from the clients'. Clients ask for consultation because they have a need for action and information. (Sometimes the consultee only needs help in taking no action without feeling guilty.) Although the consultant may be asked only for information, it is generally needed for use within a given set of circumstances. If the client really only needs information, the consultant can direct him to resources such as libraries, data services, or market research organizations.

Rule number two for consultants — **Be visible.** Many consultants do advertise and market their services. The author's experience has been, however, that word-of-mouth referrals and personal contact are the best approaches to initiate consultative contracts. Potential clients seek out consultants who are known and who are visible. One way to become both visible and credible is to be published in journals that are read by prospective clients. Articles that describe success in given situations or with specific problems are most helpful as readers can identify with them. Content articles are also useful in establishing the consultant's theoretical knowledge. Becoming known as an expert on some subject such as primary nursing, competency based education, or stress management is an excellent way to establish a reputation. (Chapter 9 describes how to get published.)

Another way to become both visible and credible is to go on the lecture circuit. (See Chapter 4 for details on getting on the circuit.) Exposure at a large national level meeting is particularly desirable since the probability of relating to specific audience needs is increased. Speaking engagements at small targeted audiences such as local chapters of the Critical Care Nurses' Association are also helpful in establishing a reputation as an expert. So, expose yourself! (Professionally, that is.)

A third way to establish credibility and capability is with testimonials from satisfied customers. Ask previous clients for letters of recommendation for use with potential clients. Remember always to get permission from the writer to do this. Telephone referrals or testimonials can also be requested. Again be sure to advise the previous client that you are going to do this.

MAKING THE CONTACT

What do you do after the request for consultative services has been made? The first step is to establish the nature and specifics of the consultation. There are several ways to do this depending on the geographical distance between the client and the consultant. A face-to-face meeting is the most desirable. If this is not possible, however, telephone is the next best way. Correspondence is the least desirable as it is time-consuming and one-sided. The author has provided a total consultation service through the mails, but it was somewhat frustrating to both parties and is not the ideal approach.

This exploratory meeting or communication is essential for mutual understanding of the service required. Don't be surprised, however, if clients are not exactly sure of what it is they want. Generally the consultant can ask the client or group to describe what precipitated the call for help. For example, was it a failure to be accredited, was it a decision to expand services, was it an increase in turnover, or was it anticipation of an organization change? Someone has said that the most appropriate time to call a consultant is when there is disagreement within a group about the ends or action plan to use to achieve a goal or objectives.

The consultant should be able, in this exploration with the client, to get a sense of whether it is problem solving, problem identification, group process or some combination of these, that is needed. Remember, the goal of consultation is to fit the service to the client's need. Don't go in with a pre-formed, already digested package deal.

The second purpose of this exploratory meeting is to begin to establish rapport with the client or group. Rapport is a fuzzy quality, hard to define, but essential to a successful consultation.

Basically, rapport means "getting along" and involves mutual trust and respect. Without positive rapport the consultative relationship may be unsuccessful and unpleasant. An experienced consultant often gets a "gut" feeling about the possibility of establishing rapport with a client. It may be better to decline a request when there is serious doubt that rapport can be established than to have the consultation end in failure.

A third purpose of the preliminary meeting is to collect any materials that will be helpful or necessary to understand the situation. The consultant may request organization charts, annual reports, audit results, staffing schedules, curriculum objectives, job descriptions, or evaluation forms, depending on the nature of the consultative service. These same materials also may be needed to write the proposal. Be sure to keep these materials and their content confidential and protected.

A fourth purpose for the exploratory meeting is to inform the client of the fees and cost for the service. Although you may not, at this initial meeting, be able to give the total cost, a range, estimated cost, or hourly rate can be given. (See Table 3–1 for factors to consider when setting fees and prices.) Many consultants do not charge for this exploratory meeting, or only charge direct expenses such as travel costs. Giving the potential client a free visit is an investment and may be a good way to establish a sense of mutual responsibility for the success of the consultation service.

WRITING A PROPOSAL

Following the exploratory meeting, the consultant writes a proposal for consideration by the client. The consultant both formalizes an understanding of the nature of the service requested, and outlines potential options. It is desirable to give a minimum of three options that vary in regard to the following variables: objectives to be achieved, time frame for achievement, and dollar cost. People like to make choices and to keep their options open. Besides, more options increase the probability that one will be selected.

The proposal should also include a description of the overall purpose of the service. This overall purpose can be extensive or narrow. Some examples of purpose statements are —

- to develop a competency-based education program for staff nurses

- to determine which nursing care system will be most effective for patients and accepted by the rehabilitation staff

- to assist faculty to clarify personal values in regard to learning, teaching, and educational methods

- to increase employee awareness of the benefits of a proposed organization change

- to discover the cause and effect of medication errors in the medical nursing department

Specific objectives are derived from the general purpose description. Details of the action plan to be used and the evaluation of achievement of these objectives are briefly described or deferred until the actual contract writing. The consultant needs to keep something back for negotiation with the client. Outline the time frame and cost for achieving each option. The consultant may also want to specify what client resources, such as space, employee time, and materials, will be required to achieve the objectives of each option. For single visit consultations the proposal may be verbal and given at the end of the exploratory meeting or telephone call.

When written, the proposal should be succinct enough so that the client gets an overall impression, but is not overwhelmed by detail. Proposals need to be flexible and succinct, so keep them to a few pages; lengthy proposals bore and confuse readers, and additional details can always be given on request. (Generally, clients look at cost first and then objectives.)

Include a cover letter with the proposal that both thanks the client for the opportunity to provide service, and states a specific day or time of follow-up. Generally, it is better to send the proposal to the client prior to a follow-up call. This delay allows the client opportunity to consider and share the proposal with others. Don't wait for the client to call you. Always follow up within a few days by telephone, letter, or a personal visit.

WRITING THE CONTRACT

The client is interested and wants to do business. Seldom are proposals accepted exactly as given. Formalizing the exploratory communication helps the client clarify his needs. Unless the consultant has "missed the boat" completely, the client requests only a few changes. Often clients will want to mix and match options, that is, take a little from one option and a little from another. The client will also ask for the details of the action plan. These implementation details need to be mutually agreed upon.

The consultant also needs to establish how often and in what form reporting should be done.

Since the fee structure was established in the exploratory meeting and in the proposal, there needs to be only a discussion of the terms of payment.

The consultant draws up a contract for the consultative service based on the discussion and client requests. There should be a written agreement even if the consultation is to be only a one-day visit. A more extensive and more expensive consultation service requires a more carefully drawn contract. Legal services are helpful and desirable for drawing complex contracts. This is business, and should be done in a businesslike way.

THE CONSULTATIVE RELATIONSHIP

No matter how well the exploratory meeting and the contract meetings have gone, there is always the possibility of something going wrong in the implementation phase. A long implementation period increases the possibility of problems occurring. Consultation is an interactive process that involves considerable give and take. Increasing the number of interactions and number of people increases the risk of failure during the process. Consider that the consultant is hired as an expert but is an outsider without authority over the consultee. This lack of authority is both an advantage and a disadvantage for the consultant who must always anticipate that the client or group may not accept the advice, suggestions, solutions, or insights offered. Conversely, the consultant cannot be "blamed" if the client doesn't follow through. A frequent consultant cry is — "Lord knows *I* did all *I* could to help them."

The consultative relationship is always temporary, even if the consultant is on a retainer. Whether it is a one-day consultation or one that lasts for several months or years, the interaction between the consultant is limited to those contacts required of the contract. Unlike a salaried staff member the consultant has access to the client only intermittently. The consultant may never even see the ultimate results of the service provided. Conversely, the consultant doesn't have to "live with" the results.

There are several distinct phases in the consultative relationship. The first is the "Getting To Know You phase." Now the consultant becomes acquainted with the client and any other individual or group who will be involved in implementation of the objectives. There could be many people involved, making it difficult to remember names, titles, and relationships. There are certain to be some "hidden agendas" and "vested interests" that can affect the implementation process. It is helpful to keep a card file of information on each contact person or group. Remember, these are for use during the consultation only and should be kept confidential and safe.

Make opportunities during the Getting To Know You Phase to inform and enlighten individuals and groups about the purpose of the consultation service, and about your credentials or qualifications. Don't assume that everyone knows who you are and what you are doing. The author has learned also to ask whether there are any forbidden subjects, materials, or locations. Few organizations or individuals want to be secretive, but there may be some sensitive subjects or places that are off-limits.

The consultative relationship involves several ethical implications. One is confidentiality. People must be sure that the consultant will not disclose or use any information about them or the organization without their consent and knowledge. Trust cannot be established without this assurance. The second ethical concern is restricting consultation to the limits established by the contract. Employees, managers or students may request additional services or use of the consultant's time. This is not appropriate unless discussed with the client. If the additional services are agreeable to the client a separate contract can be drawn, or the consultant can defer the service until after the initial contract is fulfilled. Materials developed with the client during the consultation belong to the client and should only be used by the consultant with the client's permission. Materials that are the consultant's original work should be protected with a copyright statement before being used with clients.

The "Honeymoon Phase" follows or is continuous with Getting To Know You. In it everyone (or almost everyone) is delighted that you are there, and makes you feel welcome and needed. Beware: the welcome may be for wrong reason. People often think the consultant will get some problem off their backs or will come up with some magical immediate solution. Neither is usually true.

The "Realization Phase" sets in when those involved become aware that they will have to work with the consultant to achieve the objectives. They realize this may mean extra energy, additional time, or the abandonment of some cherished beliefs and habits. This realization can be painful and threatening. The consultation may even be prematurely closed if this phase is too painful.

The "Working Through Phase" is continuous with the Realization Phase. During the Working Through period the consultant and participants strive toward achievement of the objectives. The consultant provides feedback, encouragement, enthusiasm, and expert information. Although the consultant may have been hired specifically as a content expert or as a process expert, most consultants end up doing some of both. The consultant assists clients to raise their awareness, to identify options, to acquire information, and ultimately to pursue a course of action.

During the Working Through Phase you need to be very sensitive both to progress toward the objectives and the interpersonal process. There are always overt and subtle cues that direct the consultant to press on, hold back, increase feedback, or problem solve. A consultant needs to be aware of personal biases, likes, and dislikes in order to be sensitive to the reactions of others and how to deal with them effectively.

During the Working Through Phase the consultant should provide the client with formal and informal progress reports. Formal report deadlines were agreed upon in the contract. Informal communication can be as frequent as daily depending on the nature of the service being provided. The paying client has a right to know what's happening. As a result of what's happening, the original contract may need to be revised. Unanticipated delays or problems often occur during lengthy consultations. The client and the consultant must then agree on needed adjustments and revise the contract accordingly.

Consultants often become privy to information or practices that are unknown to the client. The consultant may believe that this information should be shared with the client. However, you need to remember the importance of confidence and trust. When in doubt, always discuss disclosure with the sources and get their permission to share the information. Clinical consultants may be faced with the ethical and legal implications of unsafe or illegal patient care practices observed during a consultation service. These are difficult dilemmas to resolve.

"Closure" or "Termination" is the final phase. The relationship is ended during this phase. A long relationship usually increases the difficulty of closure. Conversely, it may be a relief to have the relationship over and done. Closure may be easier if the relationship has been successful. All parties will feel good about achieving the objectives and having a satisfying experience. Some kind of social ceremony such as a dinner or cocktail party helps to finalize the relationship in a pleasant way. The consultant submits a final report and acknowledgement letter to the client at the end of the consultation.

All of these phases may be very compressed and difficult to differentiate in a single visit consultation. They do occur however, coming quickly and simultaneously. An effective consultant is aware and alert for all of them.

CONSULTATIVE TRAPS

Even in the best of all possible worlds, mishaps occur. The usual problems of any business venture can occur in consulting. For example, collection of fees is always a potential problem; even a contractual agreement doesn't guarantee collection. The client may drag his feet in paying the fee, creating cash flow problems for the consultant. Or, the client may not pay at all, necessitating a tax write-off or legal action. Dunning clients is embarassing, tedious, and disastrous for the relationship. A formal or informal before-the-fact check on the credit and paying record of the client may prevent or minimize this problem. Obviously, another recourse in a long-term consultation is to withhold services, a losing strategy for everyone.

There is also the possibility that the contract may be cancelled. The contract may have been made with a client who leaves or falls out of favor in the organization. It may be that the problem originally precipitating the request for consultation has been solved or is no longer urgent. In such cases it is best to write off the time and effort invested and leave without recriminations. A gracious acceptance may influence the client to use you another time (if only because of guilt!!).

There are a couple of other problems or traps specifically related to the consultative role. These are:

Consultant As Dirty Guy

The consultant is hired to deliver the bad news about organization changes that result in loss of jobs or resources. Or, the consultant is put into the position of assisting a group to implement a change that was neither wanted nor agreed to by the participants. The consultant may even be represented as the originator of this change. The only consolation for the consultant is that it is a temporary role. However, should you find yourself in such a situation, you should communicate this to the people with whom you are dealing.

Hidden Agendas

This is similar to the Dirty Guy trap. The consultant is hired to achieve certain stated objectives but in reality is hired to achieve a personal goal of the client. It may be that the client wants the consultant to prove a point that was not accepted when previously made by the client. The client may want to overthrow the current administration or to discredit an incumbent, and uses the consultant as a pawn in this strategy. These ploys may backfire on the client if the consultant accomplishes the contracted objectives. The client won't like it and may penalize the consultant in some way for not helping with the hidden agenda. Here again, the best defense is to avoid such consultations in the first place or, after the fact, to communicate them to all concerned.

Lack of Commitment

The client had good intentions but, for whatever reason, doesn't come through physically or psychologically. The promised office space or secretarial help is never available. Supplies or services such as computer programming are never ordered or provided. People are never available for necessary meetings, or, if they do show up, they are obviously so stressed by other responsibilities they cannot participate. When confronted with the evidence of lack of support and commitment, the client is all apologies and excuses. Protestations of innocence and promises to do better are shortlived.

This lack of commitment from the client is a particularly vexing problem for a consultant. Even if the consultant validates the client's commitment to the goals, there has already been a delay and a break in the relationship. The only hope is an attempt to clarify the reasons for the apparent change of heart. If unsuccessful, the consultant can try to muddle through or terminate the contract.

The Consultant as Savior

Some consultants enjoy this trap and may even promote it. In this trap the client becomes dependent upon the consultant to resolve all problems. Instead of a temporary helping relationship, the consultee and consultant become enmeshed in a parent-child relationship with the consultant as the wise all-knowing parent.

This relationship may be very satisfying to the consultant's ego on a short term basis, but is a very difficult relationship to terminate without bad feelings. Ultimately the consultant is presented with problems or requests that cannot be fulfilled. The client becomes disillusioned, dissatisfied, and frustrated. Both the consultant and the client lose.

A FINAL WORD

Being a consultant can be fun, gratifying, and a terrific learning experience. As an outsider, the consultant can take risks that wouldn't ordinarily be taken in an employee role. A consultation contract often leads to other opportunities with the same or affiliated organizations or individuals. Good experiences generate additional business.

Some advice for beginners: Start small and keep it simple. Don't expect to make your fame and fortune quickly. Certainly, don't expect to support yourself initially out of your consultant earnings. Have another source of income and build your reputation slowly. Do some short-term consultations first. Remember to take on only those requests for which you have experience and knowledge. Don't overextend yourself. Be sure to allocate sufficient time for the planning as well as the implementation. There is homework associated with consultative services. You will need skills in selling and report writing. Take courses in these skills if you don't have them already.

Keep visible and current. If possible, start out by working with an already established consultant. Get a mentor, both to teach you the "ropes" and to use as a personal consultant. (Be sure to offer the mentor a fee!) You are in business, so be businesslike. You need business cards and business stationery.

A successful consultant is experienced, informed, interested in learning, enjoys working with people, is enthusiastic and, above all, is optimistic. You **have to** be an optimist to think you can make a living at blowing in, blowing off, and blowing out.

There is more involved in setting a fee for your consultative services than calculating the time spent. Not all of the items listed in Table 3-2 will be appropriate for all consultants or for each consultation. All do need to be considered at some time, however. Submit a written invoice or Request for Payment with the itemized charges or fees.

Table 3-1. Guidelines for Setting Consultation Fees

Actual time spent in consultation

Set an hourly rate, a flat fee for each visit, a flat fee for the contract or some combination of these.

The fee charged for time should be consistent with the going rate, and with what you have to offer. More experienced, better known consultants can demand higher fees.

Fees can range from $25.00 per hour to $200.00 per hour.

Time spent in getting to and from the consultation site is not usually charged to the client.

Travel expenses

Actual costs for hotel, airfare, automobile travel and meals can be legitimate additions to the fee for consultation if agreed upon in advance.

Travel expenses can also be estimated and added as a flat charge for expenses, e.g.: $50.00 per day.

If the consultation contract is a long one, a flat charge may be inappropriate as cost of travel will increase over the time of the contract.

Expenses not reimbursed by the client are legitimate deductions from gross income. Keep receipts!

Secretarial/Clerical expenses

Reports, correspondence, and written material should be professionally typed. These costs may be included in the fee if agreed upon in advance.

Secretarial/clerical expenses incurred in a consultation can also be business expense that is deductible from your gross income for income tax calculation purposes. Keep records!

The client may supply secretarial and clerical support. If so, this should be included in the contract.

The actual cost for duplication of materials can also be charged to the client directly, added as part of the flat rate, or deducted as a business expense from gross income.

Homework time

If the consultation is a complex or lengthy contract, time may be spent in preparation, investigation, or planning. This time should be considered in the fee structure.

The time spent in these activities is not usually charged to the client.

Materials

Cost of booklets, media, workbooks, tapes or equipment used with the participants can be charged directly to the client or included in the flat fee.

Materials may also be supplied by the client and will be included in the contract.

Short term or one-time consultations

These may be computed by adding the direct actual expenses to the hourly rate. Indirect expenses are considered a business expense or can be included as part of an hourly rate.

Example: 5 hours at $25.00 per hour   = $125.00
      travel to and from client   = $ 37.25
                                        $162.25

Longterm or multi-visit consultations

Compute actual consultation time plus actual direct expense plus an estimated charge for indirect expenses.

Example: 10 one-day visits at $300.00   = $3000.00
     Travel expenses @ $30.00 per day   = $ 300.00
     Estimated 15% indirect expenses   = $ 500.00
                                      $3800.00

or

Compute a flat fee that includes time spent in consultation, time spent on homework, travel expenses, and indirect expenses.

Example: Fee for Consultation Services   = $4,500.00

4 Going on the Lecture Circuit: or Taking Your Show on the Road

Dorothy J. del Bueno

T HERE IS a very old and very corny joke that goes — "You want to go on the stage? Well, there's one leaving in ten minutes."

It's not quite that easy to break into the lecture circuit or road show business. As with the consultant business, you first have to establish your credibility as an expert. In addition, you'll need to be a polished performer. The ability to perform in the entertainment sense is crucial to becoming a success "on the road." Unlike a consultant, the lecturer addresses large numbers of people, often for only a brief time. There is less opportunity to establish rapport, even if the presentation is a one- or two-day engagement. If you enjoy being "on stage," have a secret desire to be an actress or actor, and feel comfortable in front of groups you probably have the ability to become a "circuit rider." First, however, you've got to establish a reputation.

BREAKING INTO THE BUSINESS

Some of the techniques used for becoming a consultant are just as useful for becoming known as a lecturer. Publication of books or articles may lead to recognition as an expert. However, many people write better than they talk, and for lecturing you will need to develop effective delivery skills. Among the best training grounds for the lecture circuit are your local association and organization meetings. Offer your services to a local group for their next meeting or convention. Universities, colleges, and service agencies often sponsor continuing education offerings and need speakers, reactors, and moderators. Again, start small. Don't take on a whole day's presentation as your first effort. Participation in a panel discussion is less anxiety producing for a beginner. Being all alone up there can be extremely frightening.

Experience as an instructor in staff development or in a nursing school can also be excellent training for the lecture circuit. The big difference, however, is that the audience you address "on the road" is usually not a captive one, but are volunteers who don't have to be there. Therefore, they can walk out or give a damaging evaluation if you aren't good. Students and employees might also complain if you are ineffective, but their complaints won't have as disastrous an effect on your career. Remember, your survival as a lecturer or presenter depends on good ratings from the participants. Word spreads quickly about "turkeys."

An opportunity to speak at a national meeting is a plus. However, make sure you are ready. Only speak on something you are very comfortable with and have addressed before. Unless you are very experienced, the national meeting is not the place to try out a new presentation

Another way to establish yourself on the lecture circuit is to advertise. Develop a marketing piece that describes you, your programs and presentations. Go to a layout artist or an advertising agency to have the copy put into a mechanical for the printer. Some printing companies have their own layout artists, too. The point is — don't try to put the brochure together on your own — unless you have that particular expert ability. Pay for a professional job.

What do you do with the brochures after they are printed? The least successful marketing approach is a mass mailing. Most of us toss out circulars and brochures sent as bulk or second class mail. It is more effective to select a target population: organizations that provide continuing education, professional associations, or service agencies with whom you've had contact. Send your brochure with an original typed cover letter addressed to a person — not Dear Sir/Madam/To Whom It May Concern! Keep the letter succinct and follow up with a telephone call or second mailing. Probably the most effective way to market your road shows is by "P.O.P.," or point-of-purchase advertising. This is a term used to describe a method familiar from your supermarket, where there is always at least one product display at the check-out counter. While waiting, customers often pick up one of the items for purchase. Because the item is in front of a customer who is already buying something else the probability of purchase increases for the displayed item. Thus the phrase "Point of Purchase." So, when you are out on the road, in front of an audience, have your brochures with you for distribution. It is quite probable that if you have been good, future engagements will be initiated right there. As already mentioned, the best advertising is word-of-mouth from satisfied participants. "Nothing succeeds like success."

It takes time to establish yourself as a presenter. Don't expect to be able to support yourself solely on this income unless you are hired by a conference group as a salaried lecturer. If you take on this role be sure to investigate these things: What is the company's reputation? How long have they been in business? Do they get repeat invitations? Do you know anyone who has attended their programs? Are they approved, accredited, or recognized by any official organization or association as a provider of continuing education? Second, what is their financial status? Do they have cash flow problems? Are they willing to provide you with a financial statement of some kind? What is their reputation with other speakers or instructors? If the group or company is reputable and financially sound, joining it as a lecturer or instructor is a less risky way to get started.

Many lecturers, however, start out by doing this as a supplement to a salaried position. In both cases, full time and supplemental, there are ethical and contractual considerations related to being an employee. If you are working on a salary basis for a conference group you need to clarify their expectations in regard to your accepting speaking engagements requested directly of you. Do they expect you to refer this request to the group or to give them some percentage of the income from independently generated contracts? Either is a reasonable expectation since they are paying you a fee or salary — it's like having an agent.

Similarly, if you are a salaried employee of a private service or educational agency, you owe some consideration to your employer. Clarify how much time you can spend off your regular job doing your own thing. Also, clarify the financial arrangements — if the speaking engagements occur on company time do you give the money to your employing agency, split it, keep it, or make a salary adjustment? Employers are usually willing to allow employees some on-company-time to speak and give presentations as this activity is perceived as good for public relations and possibly recruitment. Just how much time needs to be agreed upon, however. (Government agencies in particular usually have strict rules and policies covering these situations.)

If you do your lecturing and road shows on your own time, you need to be sure you are still able to do what is expected on the job. It is not fair to employers to put your best effort into your "own thing" and let your salaried work suffer. Remember, should you "bomb" as a circuit rider and will need your job.

Should you decide to be a real risk taker and start your own independent conference business, read Chapter 5 on "Starting Your Own Business" carefully. It will help you avoid some of the common pitfalls.

KEEPING AND INCREASING BUSINESS

Be good!   (I.e., not virtuous, but effective.) That's the way to keep and increase your business. Being good requires both platform skills and content expertise. It must be obvious that an effective lecturer or workshop leader is well versed in the subject matter or process being presented. Know your subject inside and out, be prepared to answer questions, keep up-to-date, and revise your material based on new knowledge, discoveries, or experience. Always be on the lookout for research studies, articles, and other presentations in your subject area. The state of the art of almost every content area is constantly changing. You've got to be aware of these changes. If this is impossible, give up the act. The author, at one time, gave presentations on pharmacology. However, after a few years this topic was dropped because of inability to keep up with the literature and, even more important, because of change in job focus and practice.

Don't try to be a jack-of-all-trades! It is better to be excellent with a few topic or content areas than to be mediocre in many. Try, however, to be ahead of the trends. Be alert for new "hot" topics and develop expert knowledge and experience in them. Think of death and dying, primary nursing, staffing patterns, and competency based education. Every reader will be able to attach at least one expert's name to each of these topics. These "stars" had an edge and capitalized on being first. However, in order to survive once the trend has peaked, it will be critical to have a new topic or a variation on a theme. Has-beens are a dime a dozen.

Effective platform skills are a must for the successful lecturer. Development of these skills requires practice and more practice. The act should look easy to the audience. Entertainment isn't the primary mission, but a sound presentation is enhanced and made memorable when it is polished. Rehearse your material! Do it in front of a mirror or with a tape recorder. See how you look, listen to how you sound (remembering, however, that tape may distort your perception of how you sound). Best of all, rehearse in front of a live audience — remember the advice about starting small with a safe audience. If you use audiovisuals (and this is recommended) practice with them so you won't be fumbling and shuffling. Avoid speaking from a canned speech. Cue cards or partial sentences are more natural. If you have to use a speech, go over it enough times so that you don't have to read it word for word. Lift your head and **look at the audience!**

Time yourself! Successful presenters have a sense of timing that allows them to speed up or slow down as necessary. A minor point, but important — change your watch if changing time zones. The author vividly remembers an experience of stopping an hour earlier much to the puzzlement of the audience, because of a failure to change the time on her watch. Talk about embarassing moments — that certainly was one! Look over the facilities in which the presentation is to be given. (Potential pitfalls of the environment are described below.)

Personal style. Every speaker or workshop leader develops *a personal style.* There is no one style that is right for everyone. You should be comfortable with your own style. Some presenters are comfortable being casual, others are formal, some are witty, some are scholarly. Be natural and be sensitive to the audience. Cultivate your ability to sense boredom, apathy, hostility, and physical discomfort. Frequent short breaks are preferable to one long break — but this will depend on the nature of the presentation and the need for continuity of attention span. There are a number of techniques that help to keep an audience's attention. Some of these are use of audiovisuals (keep them short), use of humor, change in voice volume, startling statements that will challenge or invite controversy, and participative exercises.

Although your style should be natural it should be polished. Avoid heming, hawing, and repetitive phrases such as, "you-know," "well," and "that sort of thing." Your audience may end up amusing itself by counting the number of times you use your favorite phrase. Use your body language to emphasize your verbal message. Greater distance and larger numbers of people require that you broaden or exaggerate gestures for maximum effect. Remember to smile! (unless, of course you are talking about a gloom and doom subject). Maintain eye contact with different people in the audience. Use a microphone except in very small rooms or with a very small audience. A lavaliere microphone leaves your hands free to gesture, write, or change audiovisuals. A microphone also protects your voice from strain — something that can easily occur after a few hours of speaking. Voice lessons can help to increase your ability to project your voice or improve its quality. Some speakers may also need diction lessons to improve mumbling or distracting regional accents. If at all possible, avoid standing behind a podium. A raised platform or rostrum is usually necessary in a large room, but proximity to the audience usually increases effectiveness and the ability to establish rapport.

Although room size or time limits often make it difficult to establish this rapport, a speaker can certainly avoid offending or alienating an audience. Know something about them and the cultural milieu they represent. Certain kinds of jokes or stories may be offensive to some groups. Regional expressions or slang can alienate groups who don't identify with the phrasing. Religious, political, or cultural values of a given group may require that you modify your material or present it in a different context.

How you look   (see Chapter 7) is also important. Although people tend to accept more casual dress today, you need to observe some decorum in your appearance. You are on view and are trying to project an image of professional competence. Even if the session or conference is held in a resort setting, it is better to wear business clothes for your presentation. Save the bluejeans and sandals for later. Wear clothes that are becoming, conservative, and non-distracting. Solid color dresses or skirt suits for women, business suits rather than sports jackets, are better for men. Women should always wear hosiery and sleeves. Men should wear ties although ascots or turtlenecks with blazers may be acceptable in some settings. Wear shoes that are comfortable to stand and walk in, but are business-like. Loafers, sneakers, clogs, or mules are not appropriate. Women should avoid elaborate hair styles or make-up. Men need to be aware of what is generally acceptable in hair length. Don't "go native" while on stage. Muu-muus and cowboy gear might be fun and acceptable for after-hours, but are not appropriate while doing business. Even after hours you need to be aware of how your image and behavior can affect your reputation. Excessive drinking and partying can be damaging to your credibility. People want to feel you are human and real. They know we all have feet of clay — but when it starts creeping up to the knees, you're in trouble.

LOGISTICS

There are many logistical details in being a successful lecturer. Even when you are working with sponsor groups you need to be sure certain things are done. Obvious among these are travel arrangements and hotel accommodations. Getting there is not half the fun these days. Be sure to have your arrangements made in plenty of time prior to the session. Always have an alternative in case flights are cancelled. Make sure you have the right date and time on your appointment calendar. The worst thing a lecturer can do is fail to show up when expected!

The materials for the session can be duplicated or prepared by the sponsor or shipped ahead by you. Avoid having to carry a lot of handouts as they are bulky and heavy. If handouts are to be duplicated by the sponsors, give them plenty of time to do so; don't wait until the last minute to send them. Audiovisual software should be professionally prepared. Homemade is tacky! Keep an extra back-up set in case they get ruined or lost. Request equipment from the sponsor or conference management group in plenty of time.

Original instructional materials should be protected by copyright or trade-mark. There are several good articles that describe how to do this[4, 12]. Regulations change, so keep up to date. If you use other people's materials, be sure to get permission to do so. Often, participants will request copies of your materials. Whether or not you comply with this request is an individual choice. You have the right to refuse, to comply and charge for the materials, or to comply without charge. Your decision will probably be affected by your initial investment of time, money, and creativity. If you do share your materials with people be sure to clarify how they may make use of them. Don't be naive and assume that everyone knows and observes the rules and courtesies.

Many sponsors and conference managers want to give contact hours or continuing education credit for their meetings. Generally, this is their responsibility, although the speaker should be willing to provide objectives, content outline, description, brief summary, or other materials to accompany the application. Try to be as accommodating as possible, but also remember that your time is money, so don't agree to anything that will take an inordinate amount of your time.

All details in regard to length of time, program format, audience type and size and fees should be agreed upon before hand and in writing. You should also be conscientious about scheduling yourself as a presenter in competetive agencies or locations. Multiple bookings in the same location are not fair to the sponsors and will probably result in cancellation of all programs because of limited audience response. Any given area can support only a reasonable number of programs for the same or similar audience. As a lecturer, you have the responsibility to tell groups requesting your services when you have previous or future bookings in their area. Future business depends on good business relationships with sponsors.

As described in Chapter 3 on being a consultant, fee setting can be simple or complex. Table 4-1 outlines some variables to consider when determining your fee. Obviously, supply and demand is the most significant of these. Personal effectiveness, a positive reputation and a favorable image will increase your potential for larger fees. In other words, the better you are, the greater the demand will be for your services — so be good!

BENEFITS AND PITFALLS

Protecting your image is only one of the pitfalls or costs of being a star on the lecture circuit. Another, already mentioned, is the problem of becoming a has-been because "your" trend has passed or everyone has already heard it. Even worse than a worn out topic is the danger of becoming stale. Having given the same or similar presentation forty or fifty times, it is difficult to generate enthusiasm and freshness. There are several techniques you can use to avoid becoming stale. One is to vary the act. Start with questions instead of content, or use your audiovisuals in a different order. Another technique is to focus on someone in the audience and concentrate on delivering your message just to them for a few minutes at a time. Third, don't do the presentation for a period of time — take a vacation or start working on another topic. When you come back, you'll probably be enthusiastic again.

Successful lecturers travel many thousands of miles each year. Traveling isn't much fun when on a tight schedule. Nor is it

Table 4-1. Setting Fees for Lecture Services

What to charge

What you charge is related to:
- –the demand on your time
- –the market or usual rate
- –the amount of regular earning time lost
- –the amount of preparation required

–If the presentation is only an hour or two long, but requires the loss of a full day earnings in travel time, charge for at least a half day.

–If the presentation is new or tailored for the audience, requires a lot of preparative time or investment in one-time use audiovisuals, charge more or consider the time and expense as an investment.

–Anything less than $25.00 per hour is probably not worth your effort today unless you are new or are trying to establish a reputation.

–Some organizations have a policy of not paying a fee or honorarium. Free time may be written off as a charitable contribution if the organization is a non-profit one.

Other Considerations

–Establish a fee and stick to it. Generally, it is not good business to charge one group more than others. You are either worth your fee or you're not.

–Fees and expenses are usually paid after the session is given. Bill the sponsor for your services. Include receipts, bills, and a record of expenses. (Be sure to keep copies!)

–Some organizations/sponsors are slow payers. Therefore, cash-flow is often affected. Be sure to have sufficient personal funds to pay charged expenses when billed in order to maintain a good credit rating.

---

glamourous! Jet lag can sometimes be a serious health problem. One way to avoid it is to maintain regular hours even if it means going to bed at nine P.M., and getting up at 3 or 4 A.M. You can get a lot of reading or writing done that way. Eating is also a problem not only in relation to jet lag, but for weight maintenance. Invariably the lunch or dinner served at the events at which you speak will be caloric. You can request special meals, but this is a little ostentatious. Rather, try eating only the salad, vegetables and protein. Skip the rolls and dessert. Or, have a light dinner snack such as fruit and cheese on the days that you've had a heavy lunch. The author avoids airplane meals, taking an apple or some raisins instead. If you are on a special diet such as low fat, diabetic, or low fiber, alert the meeting hosts so they can make special arrangements.

Be prepared for very long and sometimes very lonely schedules. There are bound to be delays or connection problems some of the time. Learn to look for alternative methods of travel. Invest in an airline club such as Admirals or Ambassador. Membership allows you to use the lounge facilities and services. This can be very helpful when problems or delays occur. Keep your driver's license up-to-date in case you need to rent a car to get to your destination. Use a travel agent to book flights unless you have access to all the schedules and route information. Allow sufficient time to get from one place to another. There are places you can't get to directly. Make sure hotel reservations are guaranteed after 6 P.M. so you have a room when you drag into Podunck, U.S.A. at 12 midnight.

Many meeting hosts and sponsors are considerate and offer to pick you up at the airport, bring you to the hotel, or take you out to dinner. Don't expect this courtesy, however. It is a bonus. Many times you'll be on your own. Before getting into a taxi in a strange city ask if there is a flat rate or meter rate and what the cost will be — otherwise you may find yourself stuck for a $100.00 ride. Most taxi drivers are honest, but there are a few who take advantage — particularly of women!

Being a woman has additional potential pitfalls. Even today, it is difficult for a woman alone to go into a bar, hotel or a restaurant. Invariably, some masher will try to take advantage of a lone woman, particularly if she is attractive. It is assumed that she is fair "game." Hostesses and head waiters tend to give women alone the worst tables in the dining room. Room clerks give women the least desirable rooms and always wait on men first. You will need to be assertive or patient, whichever style suits you.

Hotels have their unique pitfalls. Few supply hangers suitable for hanging skirts — always bring at least one skirt hanger. All hotels seem today to have a disco or Boom-Boom Room. Invariably the room directly above this is assigned to the weary, late-arriving lecturer — you — who can't get to sleep until after 2 A.M. the time the Boom-Boom closes. If it's not the Boom-Boom Room, it's the convention participants who have really come to party, not to convene. They are always on your floor, racing up and down, laughing like hyenas, and ultimately fighting. A call to the management does no good — they won't do anything — and the hotel is booked solid. Other hotel hazards are lack of hot water, cold water, or any water, absence of air conditioning or heat, too much heat or too much cold air, fleas, water bugs (even in the best of places) and heaven forbid, bed-bugs or lice. Any or all of these are possible.

The lecturer traveling to another country can anticipate pitfalls with language barriers, customs and duty restrictions, and additional travel delays through immigration. Be sure to check if there are restrictions on use of audiovisual materials in other countries and always carry a valid passport. Carry sufficient currency of the country to pay for taxis, meals, tips, and sundries. Many places will not take U.S. dollars or even travelers' checks.

Try to find out what the weather and temperature will be like at your destination. There is nothing so uncomfortable as having clothes that are too warm or not warm enough. Open-toe shoes and a silk dress in a 35°F climate are hazardous. A folding umbrella can be very handy to have in your suitcase when going to a location like Seattle that has a heavy annual or seasonal rainfall.

Luggage can be another problem. Avoid checking baggage on airplanes if at all possible — particularly if you have to make a connecting flight. Pack sparsely. Coordinate outfits so you need, at the most, two pairs of shoes. Pack clothes that don't wrinkle, such as Ultra Suede or wool. If you use a standard suitcase, layer your clothes with tissue paper and pack tightly. A hanging garment bag carries easily and keeps clothes neater (unless there is no place to hang it up!) If you must check your luggage, be sure to hand carry your lecture materials and an overnight bag with toiletries, a change of underwear, stockings and makeup. You can at least go on stage even if your luggage is lost or is sent to San Diego when you are speaking in Chicago.

There are some "participant pitfalls" also. Usually the participants have selected your lecture or workshop because of interest in or familiarity with the topic. They are in a sense, a self-selected audience and come with positive anticipation. Occasionally, however, they may have been pressured or told to go and may resent being there. They can be resistant, perhaps even hostile. Warming up this kind of audience takes effort and sensitivity. Even worse, though, than the resistant audience, is the heckler. This person may be attention-seeking, drunk, psychotic, or some combination of the three. There is no best way to deal with hecklers. Sometimes you can simply ignore them. You may be able to divert them by requesting a personal get-together after the lecture, or you may be able to break conveniently for a few minutes. It is most important to avoid any strategy that will alienate the audience from you and lead them to sympathize with the heckler. Stay cool and professional.

A less difficult situation to deal with, but sometimes just as annoying, are participants who want to monopolize the time and the speaker. Again, never be rude or discourteous, but suggest you get together at break or lunch to discuss their particular needs. You can also ask the other participants to respond to the questions raised by this participant.

Audience size may also be a problem. A group of less than eight or ten people can be awkward for a formal presentation. If this does occur, sit down with the group in an informal arrangement and turn the presentation into a discussion. Conversely, an audience of more than 25–30 people is too large for a participative work session, unless you have colleagues to act as facilitators. Remember, these facilitators have to be prepared and expert also or it becomes meaningless. Be sure to clarify with the sponsor or host exactly what is meant by a "workshop." Without qualified leaders, group work can turn into gab sessions. Considerable skill is required both for the effective handling of both large diverse audiences and small participative sessions.

There is a whole set of potential problems related to the environment or physical setting. Murphy's Law certainly holds true — "If anything can go wrong it probably will." What are the most common of these problems? Audiovisual problems can include everything from no equipment available to equipment that doesn't work or equipment that dies in the middle of the presentation and there are no back-up parts. Room problems are infinite. Rooms can be too hot, too cold, stuffy, or too well ventilated. They can be the wrong shape or size, such as the "bowling alley" type in which you can't even see the people in the last row because they are so far away. Rooms can be too dark — everyone falls asleep — or too light — they can't see the visuals. Rooms can be too austere — no one is willing to participate — or too distracting. Your room may be perfect in every respect except that the one next to it is being used for a motivational sales meeting with cheerleading, pep-talks, and generally high volume enthusiasm. Or your room may be located next to the kitchen where they are preparing a state dinner under the direction of a very emotional, very loud chef who throws dishes when displeased.

Room set-ups can be a problem also. The classroom style inhibits participation and makes it difficult for people to take notes. An overcrowded room is as bad as an empty one. The list goes on and on! Inspect the room before your presentation so you will at least be prepared for the worst. Try to prevent problems by letting the sponsor or host know ahead of time the kind of room and seating arrangement you prefer, but be specific. The author remembers an instance when a request for an informal setting was translated into a cafeteria where eating, chatting and coming and going went on all during the presentation!

Support services can make or break presentations. If you are a polished professional your performance can be compromised by a lack of back-up. Registration should go smoothly and not run over into presentation time. There will need to be sufficient personnel there early enough to handle participants and any problems such as missing name tags, wrong names, etc. There needs to be enough hand out materials and chairs for each participant. Audiovisual equipment should be in the room and in working order prior to the presentation. As a speaker or workshop leader you should not have to take care of problems such as overflowing toilets, insufficient coffee, or coat-racks and checking service. Don't expect to be waited on hand and foot, but do expect sufficient support service to facilitate an effective session. Be flexible and reasonable — don't get the reputation as a prima-donna.

So much for the pitfalls. What are the benefits of taking your show on the road? There are several. Even though travel is not necessarily glamourous, you do get to go places you might not have a chance to visit otherwise. If possible, stay a few extra days so you get to see more than the airport and hotel. Take advantage of local tours and sight-seeing trips. Often, local people are delighted to "show off" their towns; if they offer, take advantage of this hospitality.

Traveling is also broadening — to the mind as well as the waistline! It is exciting and educational to learn what is going on in other locations, to discuss regional problems and solutions, and to acquire diverse perspectives. As a circuit rider you will learn as much from your participants as they do from you. The lecture circuit also provides the opportunity to meet many new people and make numerous contacts. Contacts can become a source of new or future business. After a time on the road, wherever you go you meet someone you've met before. It can be fun and gratifying to have so many acquaintances. Some of them may even turn out to be life-long friends or companions.

Just remember, anything can — and usually does — happen "on-the-road."

5 Starting Your Own Business

Margo C. Neal

S o you want to be in business for yourself! The fact that
nurses can even consider such an option
— let alone carry it out — is evidence that "something new" **is**
happening in the nursing profession.

The something new is that nurses are taking new kinds of
risks and assuming new roles for which they had not been prepared
or socialized. Traditionally, nurses have been socialized to work for
others — for hospitals, for physicians and for health care agencies.
Now they want to work for themselves. Since this trend can be
expected to continue, how do you go about starting a business in
nursing? What is involved in the process?

STARTING A BUSINESS IS RISKY

Do you know any nurses who have their own nursing businesses? How would you describe them? Do any of these adjectives
seem to fit?

–creative?
–independent?
–energetic?
–ambitious?

–hard-working?
–decisive?
–risk-taking?

Do these nurses seem to be a particular "type" of person? If any label is appropriate, it is definitely that of risk-taker. While there are risks inherent in any position, starting your own business is riskier than others. Essentially, there are two categories of risks, emotional and financial.

Emotional Risks

Emotional risks can be at a conscious or unconscious level. Neal[15] discussed this concept of risk-taking and made the analogy between the risk-taker and a person who jumps or falls into a flowing river. The risk-taker is willing to go a distance with the current and see what lies ahead. The non-risk-taker will grab for the first hand-hold to get out of the water. Risk-takers are often described as secure, self-confident, flexible, and adventurous.

The nurse-entrepreneur is taking emotional risks when entering a new world of unknown experiences — the business world. There are, however, ways to minimize these risks. The Aguilera Crisis Intervention Model[1] provides some specific guidelines.

Briefly, this model identifies three balancing factors that can affect emotional equilibrium. They are:

1. Perception of the event: a realistic perception of the situation helps maintain an even balance.
2. Support systems: adequate support in terms of friends, family, advisors is an important balancing factor.
3. Coping mechanisms: a flexibility that allows assessment and examination of the situation from more than one perspective is important in minimizing or "hedging" emotional risks.

When any of these factors are weak or absent, the risk of an emotional crisis increases. According to Aguilera, if any two of the three balancing factors are present, an emotional crisis (disequilibrium) is unlikely.

How does this apply to starting a business? Is your perception of the business you want to initiate realistic? Have you discussed your concept with other business people? Do they think you are realistic? Do they think you have a good idea?

What support systems do you have? With whom can you

discuss your feelings, fears, or anxieties regarding the venture? Is part of your support system someone who is in business, who has experienced a similar situation and who is willing to share some experiences with you?

What kind of coping mechanisms or options do you have? Are you flexible enough that you can devise new options, new ways of looking at ideas, at concepts? Do you have a repertoire of ways to cope with both old and new situations and with stressful situations? Are you receptive to suggestions? Can you analyze optional suggestions and recommendations and then develop a set that best fits you?

Use the Aguilera Model on an ongoing basis to assess the status of your balancing factors. Become conscious of those factors that are weak. Then take steps to decrease your emotional risk by strengthening them.

Financial Risks

The Aguilera Model provides a frame of reference for hedging the emotional risk. But how can you minimize the financial risks?

These fall into two categories, financial risks external to the business and those originating from within it. Frequently, the two overlap.

Outside risks are social, technological, and economic forces. All are major influences that bear directly on financial risks. In the 1970's, for example, the nurse practitioner movement came into its own. It continues to grow and serve an increasingly larger segment of society. Until third party payment for nurse practitioners (and nurse-therapists) is a reality nationwide, however, the potential financial risk for these nurses is considerable.

Changes in the law are significant in affecting financial risks. For instance, mandatory continuing education (C.E.) for relicensure of nurses has had an impact on all C.E. providers, and particularly those in "mandatory states." The market for C.E. in those states includes every licensed nurse in them. Theoretically, therefore, the financial risks for C.E. providers were reduced significantly.

Other external risks include natural disasters, fire, and theft.

Internal risks include inability to collect money owed, loss of a business partner, inability of the owner(s) to produce the product or service, and loss of the market or clients and customers.

Many small concerns extend credit to clients in an effort to build up business. However, if the entrepreneur does this beyond a realistic limit, cash flow can become a problem. Every business should develop a realistic credit policy. A thirty day credit period is standard. Extension beyond this limit should be allowed only for long-time customers with good paying records, or for customers with whom you negotiate special privileges. Your creditors will, no doubt, have a similar policy.

Loss of a partner can have significant negative impact on financial risk. For example, you lose a partner who does most of the creative business development. Now what? Either you try to take over that responsibility yourself or you find a replacement. In the interim the business may suffer.

Changes in the market probably contribute most to financial risk. Recall the example of the continuing education providers in "mandatory states." As soon as continuing education became mandatory, the number of providers increased dramatically. In California, in the first four years of mandatory continuing education, the number of providers rose to over 2,800. Consider the impact this increased competition had on the market. The consumer had an overwhelming number of course offerings from which to choose. Well-funded organizations were able to offer a wide variety of programs, with many fringe benefits, at a more attractive cost than could be offered by the small entrepreneur. Also, many hospitals began to offer no-fee continuing education as a recruitment and retention inducement. The competition among C.E. providers for nurse consumers intensified, changing the market totally. As a consequence, many providers, including both nurse-entrepreneurs and non-nurses, quietly folded their businesses.

It is obviously important to minimize or hedge potential financial risks. There are several ways to do this:

1. Know the current social, economic, and technological forces, as well as legislative changes, that can have an effect on your business. You can then plan for change and control the effects of the changes on your business.
2. Consult with an insurance agent regarding protection of your inventory and premises against natural disasters such as fire and theft. Make copies of all important papers, including manuscripts, proposals and presentations. Keep the copies in a separate place or rent a safety deposit box for their storage.

3. Consider contingency plans if a key person (you and/or a partner) should become ill, disabled, or otherwise unable to continue the business.
4. Develop a realistic method of collecting money owed to the business. Include a firm, realistic, credit policy.
5. Diversify your products or services as soon as possible. This is particularly important to a continuing education provider who faces stiff competition in the market place. Consider additional services or products you could provide your clients.
6. Make longrange plans considering all the risks previously outlined. Remember General Motors! Basically, GM could produce a large car for only a few hundred dollars more than they could produce a small car. They could sell the large car, however, for a few thousand dollars more than the small car. But they failed to gauge the full impact of some of the forces shaping the market, such as the rise in the price of gasoline. They therefore, lost business to their competitors who offered economically priced and economically maintained cars.

The person who is over-cautious about risks will never get a business started but, conversely, the person who takes no precautions or makes no plans to minimize risks will never be a success. The successful business-person takes a judicious stand on the continuum between these two extremes. Making the decision where to place yourself on the continuum, and moving on it as necessary, is the essence — the art and science — of doing business.

BUSINESS FORMATS: WHICH ONE?

First of all, do you have to be incorporated? Many nurses equate being in business with being incorporated, a concept no doubt influenced by the fact that most businesses familiar to nurses (pharmaceutical companies, surgical supply companies, publishers) are indeed incorporated.

You don't have to be incorporated to be in business, but you may choose to be. Bornstein[6] clearly outlines and discusses the three possible types of business formats, and the advantages and disadvantages of each. In addition to the corporation, the other two are sole proprietorship and partnership.

Sole Proprietorships

Sole proprietorships — in which one person owns all of the business — account for over 80% of all businesses in the basic industries in the US[2]. Not only is it the most common form of business, but it is also the oldest.

It is expectable that this type of business structure would be the most frequently chosen by and most appealing to nurses. One of the chief advantages of a proprietorship is the ease of formation and dissolution. It is simple and uncomplicated to initiate with few legal requirements. To dissolve, the owner simply pays off the debts owed and "closes shop." Other advantages include freedom from government regulations and tax advantages.

Businesses that start out "on a shoe string" are frequently sole proprietorships. It is a type of private enterprise and the owner is called an entrepreneur. The nurse-entrepreneur, or the nurse who has her or his own business is a new "kid on the block" in the business world.

Sole proprietorships are sometimes referred to as "DBA's." This comes from the business license required by many, if not most, cities. The license asks the name of the owner, e.g., Jennifer Smith, and the name of the business, e.g., Nursing Services. Thus, Jennifer Smith is *d*oing *b*usiness *a*s Nursing Services.

Partnerships

Partnerships are the least common of the three types of business structures. According to Altfest and Lechner[2] ". . . there are more than seven times as many individual proprietorships and almost twice as many corporations."

Like sole proprietorships, partnerships are relatively easy to form and dissolve, are subject to few regulations, and provide tax advantages.

Partnerships are formed when two or more people decide to start a business together. Frequently, the decision is a verbal one only. There are many who can state from personal experience, however, that any partnership, even the most simple, should have a written agreement. Such an agreement should include at least the following:

- the amount of money each partner will put into the business

- how the ownership will be split; e.g., 50–50

- the functions of each partner: who will do what?
- how and when profits will be distributed
- how will a dissolution of the partnership be handled, if necessary.

The idea of a partnership is very appealing. There will be at least one other person to put up money and to do the work. Most important, there will be someone with whom to talk things over, to provide emotional support and share in making and carrying out all the management decisions. Partners are liable for their share of the expenses as well as the profits, according to the terms of the partnership agreement.

Incompatibility is the primary reason for the dissolution of most business partnerships. If there is no written agreement to govern dissolution, bad feelings and bitterness can occur and frequently legal assistance is needed to settle the dispute. Bornstein[6] points out that you should choose a business partner with the same considerations that you use in choosing a marriage partner.

Corporations

Although corporations comprise only 11% of all businesses, they account for nearly 75% of the sales volume[2]. Thus corporations do dominate the business world.

Not all corporations are giant businesses, however. Many individuals incorporate their businesses in order to take advantage of tax savings and/or to protect their personal assets. (If a corporation fails, the owner is not personally liable for the debts.) A few years ago physicians were permitted to incorporate their practices, and today the majority of American physicians in private practice are incorporated. Nurses, too, can incorporate their businesses to take advantage of tax advantages and the protection of assets.

Corporations require maintenance. Like a new baby, a corporation once created must be fed and cared for. Also, initiation and dissolution of a corporation require complex and expensive legal steps. Additionally, government regulations require certain annual reports. Incorporation becomes feasible when you have sufficient assets to maintain your business and sufficient personal assets to need to protect. Many new businesses start out as a sole proprietorship and incorporate later when it becomes more realistic financially.

MONEY, MONEY, MONEY

"It takes money to make money." Since the purpose of any business is to make a profit, some financial planning is essential. To finance a business you must have sufficient cash to provide funding during that initial period when there is an outflow of money with no corresponding inflow. When you are starting out you must pay cash for such items as licenses, legal and accounting advice, advertising brochures, stationery supplies, rent, inventory and equipment. There are also maintenance costs such as salaries, utilities, and taxes. It may be several months or even years before you will take in sufficient money to offset start up and operating costs. Be sure you are adequately financed.

Sources of Support

For small business entrepreneurs, start-up money traditionally comes from the entrepreneur, family or friends who draw on savings or on personal loans from a bank. Even if you have the needed cash in a savings account, it is wise to obtain a bank loan. You may ask, "Why not use my own money and save the interest charged on a loan?" You would save the interest, but it is important to establish a working relationship and financial credibility with a bank. When you borrow from a bank and pay back the loan on time, you begin to establish such credibility. You will then be able to borrow larger and larger amounts of money as the financial needs of your business grow. You would also open your business account at the bank where you borrow money.

Another source of financial support is the Small Business Administration, a part of the US government commonly known as the SBA. The United States government actively and directly supports private enterprise through SBA loans to many small businesses.

The SBA grants loans up to $100,000, either to start a small business or to expand an existing one. In addition, the SBA provides financial counseling through SCORE, a group of retired executives who provide their services free. In 1979, the SBA initiated a new program called "Mini Loans for Women" to encourage women to get into business. These $20,000.00 maximum loans can be used to start a new business or expand an existing one.

The advantages of an SBA loan are that they carry a significantly lower interest rate than a loan made through a regular commercial bank, and a person who cannot qualify for a loan from a regular bank can often qualify for one from the SBA. The disadvantages are that SBA loans require a very large amount of paper work and they are processed very slowly. It has been said that an existing business that wants to borrow money from the SBA could be out of business by the time the loan comes through. (Doing the required paper work for a loan application, though, is an excellent and recommended exercise for anyone new to business planning.)

Other sources of financing include finance companies and business loan companies. It is important to find out their true interest rates and their payback schedules. As with everything else you purchase you must shop around to find the best "buy".

Obtaining the Loan

No bank, the SBA, or any other loan institution will lend you money because you are a nice person, because you deserve a chance, or because you have a good idea. The world is full of good ideas and good people who deserve a chance.

The bank is willing to loan money for a good idea only when the idea is backed with loan collateral and evidence of sound financial planning. The lending organization must protect its investment. It must ensure that the borrower will be able to pay back the loan, or if that is not possible, that the loan collateral will repay the loan. Collateral for a loan can be real estate (often in the form of a second trust deed), stocks or bonds, or cash in a savings account.

The bank will also be interested in your plans for the money. What are the specific purposes for the money? In order to know this yourself, you need to develop a business plan.

The Business Plan

Include in your business plan:

– the purpose of your business

– the specific goals and objectives of the company

– a definition of the products or services you will sell

– a proposed budget: projected expenditures (cash outflow) and income (cash inflow) for the first six months of business and, in less detail, for the next three years

– delineation of your market

– personnel

The SBA has an excellent booklet to help you develop a business plan, "Checklist for Going Into Business." It is available at no charge from your local SBA office or from the SBA, 1441 L Street, N.W., Washington, D.C. 20416. It is highly recommended that you send for this booklet and follow the instructions for developing your own written business plan. Developing such a plan will be of great help to you in organizing and starting your business even if you don't plan to seek a loan. As in any other endeavor, sound planning will pay large dividends. Other people can give you input and critique your plan but, it is important that you develop the plan yourself.

TO MARKET, TO MARKET, TO SELL . . . WHAT?

What do you have to sell? And to whom? Any entrepreneur — nurse or otherwise — who considers starting a business needs to have a good idea of (1) what is to be sold, and (2) who will buy it. Without clear delineation of the products or services and the buyer, further planning may be an exercise in futility.

> Traditionally, nurses . . . . have . . . . had minimal involve-
> ment with marketing . . . . Like many professionals and
> others in nonprofit, service organizations . . . . they have
> associated marketing with profit-making, commercial en-
> terprises that sell soap, cars, or television programs[11]."

Arleen Gordon, in the article from which this quote is taken, provides an excellent overview of basic marketing principles with specific application to continuing education. She points out that attitudes toward professionals are changing. For example, lawyers now advertise and there have been radio ads for a visiting nurse association.

Marketing is essential. No business can survive without it. The degree and amount of marketing necessary will depend on the products and services offered for sale and the potential customers.

The Marketing Mix

A basic model of marketing delineates "four Ps:" the prod-uct, the price, the place, and the promotion. Together they are called "the marketing mix."

The product is what you have to sell. If your business is a clinical practice, then you sell a service. People who provide continuing education programs are selling an educational service. A consultant's product is also a service. Businesses that sell books or forms have a tangible product to sell. Some businesses have both services and tangible products.

Once you have decided what it is that you will sell, then you need to define it further. Answers to these questions will help you in this process:

1. If your business is a clinical practice, what are its parameters? Will you have a generalized or a specialized practice (eg., psychotherapy, cardiac rehabilitation, general medical clinic or nutrition counseling)?
2. Where will you practice? In your office? The client's home? A doctor's office?
3. Who is apt to buy your product? Is it a particular age group, e.g., geriatric clients? Will you sell your continuing education programs to a hospital, a temporary staffing agency or to individual nurses?
4. When will your product be available, that is, will you have specific hours? Will your educational programs be monthly, weekly? How much inventory will you have on hand to avoid delays in filling orders?
5. Why have you chosen this product? Is there a similar product or service available? If so, how will yours differ? Is there a need and a desire for it? Be aware of the difference between the two. For example, a group of nurses may *need* a continuing education class in fluid and electrolyte balance but they may not *want* it. They may want a class in stress reduction and consequently will buy the latter.

The selling price must cover both the cost of production (including your time) and the cost of marketing, and provide a reasonable profit. Price is also affected by what the customer is willing to pay. What is your competition charging?

The place refers to the way you will distribute your product. If you are providing a service, then distribution does not apply because you are delivering the service directly to the client.

If, however, you want to distribute a product nationwide, you need a distribution channel. Some distribution channels are:

selling your product directly to a national chain; selling to a distributor who will in turn sell your product to numerous outlets within his geographical region; and selling your product to the consumer via direct mail.

Promotion is a vital aspect of any business. Traditionally, professionals did not need or want promotion. They just "opened their doors" and clients came. But, times are changing. The field is becoming crowded. *The Los Angeles Times* recently carried an article about a dentist in the San Francisco Bay area who uses promotional techniques to attract clients. His clients are primarily children, so he wears various costumes for his clients. One of the more popular costumes is "Plaque Vader."

Promotion not only brings clients and consumers to the business, but it also describes the features and benefits of the product or service. Such information is demanded by consumers today; they want to make *informed* choices. Some *kinds of promotion* are:

– "Word-of-mouth" — one person tells another. Positive word of mouth advertising is the best promotion you can have. But it won't come until you have a track record.

– Public relations — any effort that serves to create a positive image of you and your business with the public. An excellent way to obtain this is to talk at various group meetings at no charge. Some groups you may want to consider are church groups, women's groups, medical groups, or any community function. Depending on the make-up of the group, you may talk about your specific services (e.g., speaking to a group of physicians about your home dialysis service) or about your area of expertise (e.g., speaking as a psychotherapist about life crises to an adult community group.) Volunteer to serve on committees, to be a part of a conference program, or offer to subsidize a coffee break at the conference.

– Sales promotion — the use of premiums, contests, or bonuses to help sell a product or service. Sales promotions are relatively easy to develop when you are selling a tangible product ("buy one book, get the second one at half-price") but more difficult when selling a service. Extra copies of reports or charts or additional consultative visits could be promotional items for services. If two businesses offer exactly the same service, a promotional item could be the deciding factor in getting the customer.

– Advertising — placing ads in local newspapers, on radio or in trade journals. The advantage of this type of advertising is that it will reach a large number of people at a relatively low cost. Advertising by direct mail allows you to target a specific group of people who are likely to buy your product. A "good" response from an initial direct mail campaign is 2%. That means the mailing needs to be large to be profitable. Direct mail is a specialty business in itself; learn more about it from an expert before taking the plunge.

Your Marketing Plan

Just as you need a business plan, you also need a marketing plan. Don't expect people to flock to your door just because you are open for business. And don't plan on other nurses' patronage just because "we're all nurses." It doesn't work that way. Like other consumers, your colleagues will patronize you if you have a good product or service that they want.

A basic marketing plan will include answers to the following:

– What specifically do you have to sell? How does it differ from the competition?

– Why should the public buy from you rather than from someone else?

– Is there any competition? Who are they? Is the market large enough to support several businesses of the same kind?

– Why do you think people will buy the particular product or service you offer? Is it something they "have to have" or something it "would be nice to have?"

– What will you charge? Again, find out what the competition is charging; consider your own costs of production.

– How will you promote your product? What specific steps will you take to get your message out to the public? Plan your public relations and/or advertising. Do you need ad-

vertising brochures that will explain your business to potential customers?

You can expect that your overall marketing plan will change
with the circumstances. However, development of an initial marketing plan will be a significant help as you organize your business.

PULLING IT ALL TOGETHER

That's just what you need to do in order to get your business
off the ground. It must be evident by now that starting a business
involves a great deal of effort on your part. There is homework to
be done, things to be learned, information to be found, people to
contact, and on, and on, and on. Of course, you must also decide
if this is really what you want to do. If the answer is affirmative,
start the groundwork.

Groundwork involves developing both a business plan and
a marketing plan. A great deal of printed information is available
to help you with this process; from the SBA, from the Bank of
America, from a library, or from books obtained from the business
section of any good bookstore. Check out universities and colleges
for workshops and classes. Scan the papers for upcoming lectures
and seminars. There are many education opportunities available in
larger cities.

You will need human resources too. How do you know
which CPA, which attorney, to consult? You will need both. There
is no one easy answer but a few tried and true methods are recommended:

1. Do you already know people — an attorney, a CPA
— who perform the services you need? Or do you know someone
who can recommend others? As with everything else, you need to
shop around and find people whom you consider competent, and
with whom you feel comfortable.

2. Join an organization of business people. The members can
supply you with references, recommendations, and support. In addition, you can explain your business to them, and offer referrals
and references in return. For men, traditional organizations include
the Kiwanis, Rotary Clubs, and the Chamber of Commerce. There
are no traditional groups for women but within the last five years,
many have sprung up. The Women in Business group in Los Angeles is an example.

"W.I.B." grew out of a women's workshop at University of

California, Los Angeles. The participants wanted to continue the support and information exchange that occurred in class. Today, W.I.B. is an active organization of several hundred corporate and entrepreneurial women. The organization provides support in many ways to its members. It also provides seminars to the community helping other women who are just starting out in business. Most large cities now have one or more such groups. Seek them out and visit them.

3. Talk to business people, starting with those you know and respect. Tell them what you want to do and ask them for suggestions and ideas. Invite them to lunch. It is a nice gesture and good business!

4. Specifically, take another nurse-entrepreneur to dinner. Most recent nurse-entrepreneurs made it without the support of other nurses, other organizations, and certainly without the support of educational preparation. Most will be willing to share at least some of their experiences with you. But, don't be naive and expect other entrepreneurs to share all of their business practices with you just because you are all nurses. And certainly don't ask advice from a nurse-entrepreneur whom you expect to be your chief competition. Can you imagine anyone going to MacDonald's and asking for help in setting up a competitive hamburger business?

Once you have made the basic decisions as outlined in your marketing plan and developed your business plan, you are ready to begin to implement them. You will need to do all of the following.

1. Obtain space. Will you have an office, or work out of your home? A separate telephone number is probably advisable.
2. Obtain a business license if required. Check with your city hall.
3. Open a bank account that is separate from your own personal account. Establish your credit and your financing.
4. Set up some type of bookkeeping system. It can be a simple system such as a ledger you buy at your local office supply, or a more complex one that is set up and maintained by a bookkeeping service. You may choose to have a system that is developed by you in conjunction with a CPA.
5. Have business cards and stationery printed.

6. Set a target opening date. How long will it take you to prepare, to be ready for customers?
7. Determine how much time you can reasonably allocate to your endeavor. If you are well-financed, you may be able to devote 100% of your working time to it. If you are not well-funded, you may have to hold down a part-time job that will ensure a steady income.
8. Arrange for support services such as tying, telephone answering, or mailing services.

AND OVERALL. . . . .

Starting a business is an exciting venture. It gives you tremendous freedom to create what you want and to do things the way you feel they should be done.

The many preparatory activities should fall into place once you have made the basic decision to do it! Like the proverbial snowball, once it starts rolling, your business can get bigger and bigger. As you become more experienced, you will devise new practices and new products that will undoubtedly be very different from your original ones. That is how businesses grow — they change and adapt to the times and customs.

The 1980's are a good time for nurses to be going into business. The climate is right. Although still only a very small group, it can be expected that the number of nurses in business will increase dramatically in this decade. The challenge is there. It's a lot of hard work but also exciting, rewarding, and satisfying.

. . . and for a salesman, there is no
rock bottom to life . . .
ARTHUR MILLER
DEATH OF A SALESMAN

6 Opportunities in Sales

Anthony S. Alfieri

AM I A CANDIDATE?

MANY WOMEN have considered the possibility of a sales career but become frightened at the thought of entering a "man's world." Historically, sales evokes an image of a back-slapping, cigar-smoking individual telling jokes and incessantly talking. Or, of the stereotype of the door-to-door salesman pushing his way into the privacy of your home, trying to sell something you don't need such as a vacuum cleaner or a set of encyclopedias. Then there's the other stereotype, the salesman with the loud suit and sunglasses selling a used car and promising you a world of benefits at $200 less than any other dealer in town. It's easy to understand why a woman would hestiate to embark on a career in sales with those perceptions of her fellow salesmen. Like most stereotypes, however, these do not reflect today's reality of an effective salesperson.

What does it take to become a good salesperson? There are some basic traits that are required for success. First you need what motivation. Is it financially necessary that you work? Financial obligations are a strong motivating force. If you have to pay off a car loan, the monthly rent, food bills or tuition, and have no other source of income there will be a need to work and to be a success.

The ability to earn a substantial salary also provides feelings of financial independence and importance, two ego needs that today's women desire to satisfy. Society unfortunately often defines success by amount of money accumulated rather than the quality of a person's education, culture or intellect. However, financial gain can be the motivating force that makes you successful in a sales career.

A successful saleswoman enjoys meeting people and facing new situations. She enjoys building social relationships through contact with people during the normal course of a day. A successful salesperson loves competition whether in tennis, golf, bridge, chess or anything providing an opportunity to exhibit self-confidence and the ability to win. If you are competitive you probably also hate to lose. Self-confidence is critical to successful selling. It influences the buyer to trust you and have faith in you. Confident saleswomen have little difficulty in selling the benefits of their product or service.

All successful saleswomen are winners, but if they do lose a sale they don't lose self-confidence. If you are a person who continually doubts your own worth when you fail, a career in sales is not for you. An effective saleswoman learns from failure. She analyzes the sales presentation and the background knowledge of her customer making every effort to improve upon previous mistakes. To be a successful saleswoman you have to look past disappointments and try again and again. Vince Lombardi, the famous coach of the Green Bay Packers, once said, "Winning isn't anything, it's everything." That is the philosophy of many successful sales people.

How would your closest friends describe you? If their description includes the words unethical, insensitive or deceptive, then you probably can anticipate an unsuccessful sales career. But, if your friends describe you as persevering, industrious, compulsive or even egotistical, then with some training and practice, these traits can be turned into positive selling strengths.

Salespersons usually like to be active. They prefer active participation to passively watching others. They may watch for a while simply because they're unfamiliar with the activity but, once familiar, they have the confidence to become involved without fear of failing. There is an old adage that relates to the active participant: "Some people wish things would happen. Some people watch things happen. Other people make things happen." The successful sales person always makes things happen.

Do people confide in you? Are you easily persuaded? Can you carry on a telephone conversation comfortably, without becoming tense? How do each of these questions pertain to a sales career? People who confide in you are vulnerable. Ordinarily they will do so only if they trust or value your advice. If you are the kind of person people confide in, prospective customers will probably trust you with their business needs. A trusting relationship often leads to a profitable relationship. Conversely, do you find yourself being easily persuaded by your friends, peers or family? The next time you have the opportunity, try to convince someone to go to a place other than the one that was planned. Try to persuade your family to taste a new recipe by making a new epicurial adventure sound enticing. The ability to persuade prospective customers or consumers is the critical element in successful selling. This is not easily achieved. Customers usually challenge and put up barriers or obstacles. You must overcome these challenges by being the persuader instead of the one persuaded.

How good is your telephone personality? Many prospective buyers require appointments for sales presentations. Since many appointments are made by telephone, how you use the telephone is very important. Many times that first telephone call makes the difference between success and failure. You may feel very comfortable talking to someone face to face. But, are you as comfortable on the phone? Anxiety or uneasiness can be conveyed over the telephone to the party on the other end. You may seem less personable or convincing than when face to face. If you can put your customer at ease over the telephone, you will be successful at making appointments.

Now that you have a better understanding of the characteristics needed to be a successful saleswoman, make every effort to improve those in which you are not already competent. Ask your friends to help evaluate your progress. Accept the fact that you need to improve, but don't be immobilized. Use your strengths to be positive as you enter the exciting and challenging field of sales. "You can break traditional barriers." "You can do it if you really want to." "I have a lot of faith and confidence in you." "Don't let other people stop you." Do these phrases sound like your mother? For years mothers have been "selling" to their children and their husbands. Remember Eve? She persuaded Adam to eat the apple. Selling is, without a doubt, a woman's game. Women traditionally have been socialized to attend to others, to indulge others, and to give pleasure to the users and takers. Since selling involves satisfying the needs of the other person as well as one's own desires, a woman's innate sales ability needs only to be developed. One of the greatest feelings on earth is winning at the selling game. As a woman you deserve to win more than anyone else.

WHAT CAN YOU EXPECT?

Statistically women comprise 40% of the work force in the United States. Of this 40% only 6% hold middle management positions. On the average, women are paid 25% less than men, an insulting disparity. One way to correct this inequity is to set out to make a successful invasion of the traditional purviews of the man's world.

A sales career is a potential stepping stone to management. There is no limit to the advancement opportunities for successful, motivated salespeople who set longterm goals and priorities. Ask yourself what you would like to be earning and what sales position you'd like to hold next year, two years from now, and over the long haul.

The types of sales opportunities differ. Certain industries afford a quicker path to success than others. Conversely, there are industries with long-term potential growth, providing greater monetary rewards and benefits. For example, in a small company you would begin as a sales representative. Advancement would be first to sales manager, then vice-president of sales and then, finally, president of the company. In a large Fortune 500-type corporation there are more stepping stones. In a large company you start out and remain a general sales representative for several years, then move on to be a specialty representative for important or national accounts. Then, depending on your success and recognized potential for management, you can progress to assistant manager, district manager, regional manager, vice-president of sales or marketing, president, and finally chairman of the board. Obviously, the career path in a large corporation requires more years in each position and considerable competition with others who are also trying to succeed.

There are many industries in which a nurse might pursue a sales career. Among those affording the greatest opportunities are insurance, electronics, space, brokerage firms, fashion, office furniture, industrial sales, pharmaceuticals, real estate, publishing and cosmetics. It may seem smart to select an industry that fits your particular educational background. A registered nurse might gravitate to the pharmaceutical or hospital supply industries because of familiarity with medications and hospital products. However, applicants participating in corporate sales training programs were highly successful on completion of the course even without prior product knowledge or familiarity. Many industries even prefer inexperienced sales people because they have not formed any bad selling habits. Corporate sales trainers then have the opportunity to program the trainee to the selling techniques advocated by their sales managers. Many large corporations have excellent sales training programs which prepare representatives for the "real world" of selling. So, don't be afraid to enter an industry that appears, at first glance, inappropriate or unfamiliar. Remember, selling is primarily building relationships and filling the needs of prospective customers, goals already familiar to nurses. Getting the job you want in sales requires the same approaches and strategies used in obtaining a job in nursing. (See Chapter two for pointers on applying and interviewing for jobs.)

Your first job in sales should not be your last. Moving from job to job increases your risk-taking skills. You can accumulate varied experiences that can then help you decide on a specialized sales field. Make each move more financially profitable by thoroughly investigating the track record of your new employer. Some of the factors that should assist you in choosing a new company are starting salary and benefits such as vacation, medical and dental health plans, bonus and commission arrangements, life insurance, tuition plans and pensions. Ask your potential employer questions about the amount of travel and travel expense, promotion opportunity, relocation practices, training, size of sales force and most important, the company's attitude toward women. You can then make a more intelligent decision based on facts instead of assumptions.

There are some benefits that are peculiar to sales positions, including advances, commissions and bonuses. Unlike other jobs where there may be financial discrimination for a woman's productivity, a sales woman is paid the same as a salesman. If the position pays a 10% bonus or an 8% commission then every salesperson receives the same reward for the same sales achievements.

Industrial selling generally offers the opportunity to earn more money than most other sales jobs. However, there are no hard figures to document the range of earnings in sales at the present time. David King, a sales expert and founder of Careers for Women, states that, if you are average, you'll earn $25,000 a year by the time you're finished with the first three years of your selling career. Many salespeople can earn yearly salaries of $40,000 and $50,000 after five or six years' experience[13]. Salary does depend on the type of industry, a corporation's guidelines and most important, your actual sales achievements. Before accepting a sales job, determine the salary you expect to earn and be realistic in your expectations, to avoid being disenchanted or disillusioned later on. Although offering good career potential, selling is not usually the best way to accumulate wealth rapidly. There are other high risk ventures you can enter if you are interested in get-rich-quick schemes.

Some salespersons, particularly clerks or order takers, find selling boring and routine. They perform the same tasks with the same people in an unchanging environment, constantly fighting monotony. Other sales people are not very happy because they don't like the products they are selling or don't believe in the manufacturer's claims. These people may feel that the product does not satisfy the customer's needs. Such feelings are common and may be experienced by any salesperson. They are, however, less common in industrial sales because of the stimulating challenges in this area. Industrial salespeople get to meet many new and different people every day. In industrial selling you are given a territory and the freedom to manage it your own way to achieve the required sales quota. There is very little daily supervision. This allows you to be creative in your selling, basing your approach on analyses of your customers' problems. You determine a solution that will culminate in a sale. The opportunities are endless because of the many different customer needs. The successful salesperson is flexible, modifying the sales approach on almost every call. These ever changing situations and challenges prevent boredom and provide for creativity.

The sales and business world is filled with ambiguities. You will find that management directives are often confusing and are constantly changing. You may find that your views are directly opposed to and in conflict with your sales manager's viewpoint. You will sometimes receive what seem like illogical instructions that inhibit your sales achievement; coping with these ambiguities is a necessary element of success.

Management is primarily interested in your ability to get the job done. You don't necessarily have to work hard in sales but you do need to work "smart". The job must also satisfy *your* ambitions and needs or you won't be happy. Although the achievement of personal goals such as increased income, status and even power is not unique to a career in sales, it does present a greater likelihood of attaining them.

HAZARDS TO SUCCESS

Steward Emery, a humanist wrote, "The world is divided into two kinds of people: the people who are fearful and can't move ahead and the people who are fearful and take their fear with them [8]." Many sales candidates are frightened at the thought of being unsuccessful in a new job. They are often paralyzed into a state of inactivity. Remember, any worthwhile activity has the risk of both success and failure.

What is success for you? Is it the amount of money you accumulate? The number of degrees earned? The business position achieved in a lifetime? Everyone has a different interpretation for success. You are truly successful when you honestly believe you are.

What are the common pitfalls of selling? Lack of commitment is most hazardous if you are going to sustain a successful career in sales. You must be committed. You are given a territory and the responsibility to sell a service or a product. Lack of commitment to this responsibility will result in poor sales, inability to meet your quota and failure. You won't, of course, win all of your sales attempts. Some customers may turn you down or take their business elsewhere. Accept these rejections and learn something from them. Use these rejections to identify skills needing improvement. Don't take rejection or failure personally. It is not you the customer is rejecting, it's your product or your sales presentation. With perseverence you will make things happen in your territory that will give you the incentive to go on to greater sales successes. It is not easy and it will take time. Getting the sale comes only through committed effort. If you are an overachiever you may accomplish your goal beyond your wildest expectation.

Another hazard to success is the inability to be self-directed. Most nursing programs are based on a structured curriculum with mandatory courses leading to a degree or diploma. A graduate nurse in a hospital setting is generally expected to function within a set of guidelines, standards, and medical orders; the job is part of a structured experience.

The business world and a sales career are very different from most nursing experiences. The freedom of a sales territory, the lack of supervision, and the responsibility to manage your customers may be difficult and even frightening. If you prefer a very structured and highly supervised environment then you may have difficulty coping with the independence required. Some of you may think you need more supervision than usually provided because of lack of experience. This is a normal reaction to a new career in unfamiliar surroundings, requiring new relationships, but with or without experience it is ultimately your ability to function effectively without structure and supervision which will determine your success. There is no time clock and no one calling when you don't show up in your territory. You must be self-directed, self-motivated, and disciplined. However, nurses have an excellent foundation for success in selling because of their skill in relating to people, being sensitive to peoples' needs, and following up on cues given during interactions. These background skills, combined with on-the-job experience, will restore and enhance the self-confidence needed to overcome the anxiety of an unsupervised freedom.

A third hazard, related to commitment and self-direction, is lack of motivation. Motivation, or the will to win, is what separates the girls from the women, and the champions from the also-rans. Successful salespeople improve on their innate abilities and minimize their weaknesses. Motivation requires a tremendous amount of energy, pushing ahead even when discouraged or tired. Motivation is when you do what you are doing because the job or what it represents is important to you. Sales quotas and bonuses may move you to be an effective salesperson, but motivation will make you great.

A fourth hazard to success is lack of "hustle." Successful salespeople are expected to hustle. What is hustle? Sally Moore, a successful real estate saleswoman, defined it this way.

> Hustle is doing something that everyone is absolutely
>   certain can't be done.
> Hustle is getting the sale because you got there first or
>   stayed with it after everyone else gave up.
> Hustle is getting prospects to say yes after they've said no
>   twenty times.
> Hustle is doing more for the customer than the other guy
>   is doing.
> Hustle is hating to take a vacation because you might miss
>   a piece of the action.
> Hustle is heaven if you're a hustler, and hell if you're
>   not[7].

If you can't hustle, at least most of the time, you'll probably be unsuccessful in sales.

How tough are you mentally? If you can't take rejection you can't be successful in sales. Customers often put seemingly insurmountable obstacles in the way of your sales success. Such obstacles may stimulate emotions of anger, resentment, and despair. If you allow these normal emotions to immobilize your efforts or cause you to give up, you will not succeed. To the successful salesperson, obstacles are opportunities. As Bud Wilkinson, a football coach at the University of Oklahoma said, "when the going gets tough, the tough get going."

Sales managers evaluate representatives on their ability to overcome obstacles to success. They expect salespeople not to back off from opposition. Conversely, they also expect the salesperson to recognize when it is better to walk away gracefully from a hopeless situation rather than antagonize a customer and thus close the door to future sales presentations or strategies. Being tough doesn't mean being aggresive, insensitive, or belligerent. Rather, it is similar to being assertive. A female chauvinist can be just as unpopular as a male chauvinist.

Successful selling depends on relationships with people. You must be socially astute, and have acceptable social skills. You will need to be acceptable to your customers. How you look, talk, and act will influence this acceptance. (See Chapter 7 on Image). In our society, women are generally better prepared for social situations and small talk. Many times both men and women find it easier to discuss problems with an understanding woman. Women are not burdened with machismo, a quality that inhibits sensitivity to others' needs. Some saleswomen have mistakenly believed that to be successful they should repress these womanly or feminine characteristics and act, think, and talk like men. Act like a successful woman, not like a woman trying to look like a successful man.

Lack of loyalty is another hazard to success in business. In business you are expected to follow the company line and stay within its policies. You are expected to obey orders and to temper any objections or questions with diplomacy. As a loyal employee you are expected to defend with enthusiasm your company and its products or services. You are expected to keep "dirty linen" within the confines of the company. You may even be expected to be available, at least by telephone, twenty-four hours a day, seven days a week. Personal affairs should be secondary to company business. If you are constantly challenging company values and practices, you may be labeled a rebel or misfit and compromise your chances for promotion. These expectations, not really different from those in many health care agencies, may seem unreasonable. Nevertheless, it is important to future success to be perceived by management as a company person and a team player.

SALES AND SEX

Chances are that as a saleswoman, many if not most of your buyers will be men (unless, of course you are an Avon lady or Sara Coventry salesperson). Sooner or later the problems of being a woman will surface. They can be related either to sex or sexism.

If you are an attractive, charming, warm woman you can expect to be approached, propositioned, or touched. When a male makes a sexual advance he believes he is paying you a compliment. How will you handle these approaches? Carefully — if you don't want to alienate a customer. A rebuff can be straightforward yet tactful. Be sure your response is sincere and given early in the encounter, otherwise you can be accused of being a tease or leading the customer on. Some women may choose to use their sexual attraction as a strategy to get a sale. There is a risk in either allowing yourself to be blackmailed into giving sexual favors or in making sexual promises to close the deal. If you can't sell your product or service on its merits and value to the customer, you probably won't last too long as a salesperson. David King and Karen Levine in their book, *The Best Way In The World For a Woman To Make Money,* describe some excellent strategies to use in handling sexual advances[13].

Most of your fellow salespeople and your boss may also be men. Most people will advise you that sex and business don't mix. This is especially true when the man who is attracted to you or vice-versa is your boss. If your success in the company depends on your sexual relationship with your boss, or his boss, it may be very uncertain. Discretion and professionalism are important to your credibility inside and outside the company. Although position may be everything in life, the position for a saleswoman should be vertical at all times!

Sexism is a different problem. Sexism is discrimatory behavior or activity because of the person's sex. You, however, are not one of the boys and should accept that there will be times when you won't fit in or will make the men feel uncomfortable by your presence. If you are single it may also be difficult to fit into the planned activities for spouses at meetings or the outside social commitments expected of the sales force. Use good judgment. Don't try to participate in all of the activities, such as the poker games or out-on-the-town jaunts after the sales meeting. You should however, be treated as an equal in regard to bonuses, quotas, assignments, and salary. You should not be discriminated against for promotion because you are a woman. Neither should you be favored as a member of a minority group. For success maximize your feminine strengths and minimize the limitations inherent in being a woman in a man's world.

SUMMARY

This chapter has described the opportunities in sales, the characteristics required for success, and the potential hazards to success. A successful saleswoman will also have to acquire and develop the how-to's of selling. Most companies will provide on-the-job training, sales courses, and continuing education. You will find also that there are many excellent books, articles, and courses on selling techniques. Take advantage of any opportunity to learn new skills. Seek advice and suggestions from experienced successful salespeople. Capitalize on your previous knowledge of psychology and communication skills. Get a mentor who will help you learn the politics in the company.

Selling, like nursing, is a strategy used to meet peoples' needs. It is only the focus and the context of the strategy that is different. If you are a successful nurse who enjoys a challenge, who can overcome obstacles, and who likes freedom and flexibility you will probably be successful in sales. Try it, you'll like it.

III INVESTING IN YOURSELF

7 Image and Appearance You Can't Judge a Book by Its Cover — or Can You?

Dorothy J. del Bueno

THERE'S AN old saying — you can't judge a book by its cover. That may be true, especially with paperbacks. However, it is equally true that first impressions are important and may be lasting. Clothes may not make the man (or woman) but appearance and presentation of self are important factors in personal image and success.

WHAT IS THE SIGNIFICANCE OF APPEARANCE?

Values about appearance are, like all values, formed at an early age and difficult to change. Consider the never ending difference of opinion about whether or not nurses should wear caps and white uniforms! Remember how vigorously parents and managers in the sixties reacted to the long-haired sloppy "hippy" look? History books describe how outraged society was about the first men who dared to change from knee britches to those ridiculous trousers. Museums show exhibitions of clothes through the ages, recording the changes in fashion and style that are often reflective of moral values, economic trends, and social change. Skirt length supposedly is related to financial recessions and depressions with hemlines going down with economic decline. Waist lines and necklines rise and fall and seem to parallel attitudes towards sexual promiscuity. Compare, for example, the high waists of the Edwardian age and Regency periods with the Victorian waistline and hoopskirt. How one looks is a reflection of important cultural values and may be as important as the values related to child rearing and religion.

A successful woman acknowledges fashion trends and cultural expectations and adapts her appearance accordingly, at least while in her business or professional role. This does not mean, however, slavish adherence or a complete makeover. Total immersion in fashions is as foolish as total ignorance of what is in style.

COSTUME CAMEOS — ARE ANY OF THESE FAMILIAR?

The Prom Queen. This woman was the belle of the ball when she was in high school or college. She continues to wear her hair in the same style she wore then. Depending on her present age, it could be the pompador, the pageboy, or the long, straight ironed look. Her clothes are juvenile, often ruffly, and cutesy. You can practically hear the cheerleaders and Lester Lanin in the background.

The   Gypsy. Bangles, beads, flowing ringlets, yards of skirt and brilliant colors are the trademark of this type. Colorful yes, successful no — unless doing business in Romany. All she needs is castanets.

The Dowd or the Poor Relation This woman is the antithesis of the gypsy. She believes that people shouldn't care about how she looks, but only about what she does. Thus, she eschews all trends and fashions and wears whatever is hanging in the closet. She's clean, but not very esthetic; sincere, but certainly not stylish. Knee socks with a chemise, striped wool jacket with a flowered dirndl skirt — it's all the same to her.

California   Casual — Also Known   as — The   Camper. Wholesome, healthy, bursting with vitamins and the great outdoors. Down vests, sandals, or a man's shirt are part of every outfit. When she does decide to dress up it's a skirt and blouse or shift. No makeup or frills for this nature girl.

The   Preppy. Tweed hacking jacket, penny loafers, pleated skirts, crewneck sweaters and oxford cloth shirts — these are all well coordinated and look great for a weekend in the country — but not for the meeting with the board or the annual hospital dinner. This woman's taste is conservative but not always appropriate.

The Show-Girl. Exactly the opposite of the preppy. The show-girl looks ready for Hollywood and Vine or the Broadway stage. Heavily made-up, she wears sexy outfits of clinging fabrics with low necklines and usually lots of jewelry. Her hairstyle is elaborate and heavily sprayed. This woman attracts attention, but not necessarily the right kind.

These descriptions may be somewhat exaggerated but unfortunately do exist. Taste is a highly individual and personal matter. However, how you look reflects your persona and does have an effect on others' first impressions. If your personal image is distracting or offensive it may prevent the development of an effective working relationship. People are often so "turned off" by appearance that they find it is difficult to concentrate on what is happening or what is being said. People may conclude that an individual who presents an offensive appearance has no respect for them. The successful professional woman's appearance is a combination of what is becoming, what is in style, and what is consistent with the values of the people with whom she associates professionally.

Image and Appearance

The military, the church, and the law enforcing agencies all recognize the influence dress and appearance have on others' behavior. Many New Yorkers have concluded from their observation of a new laxity in appearance of New York's police force that civilization, (or at least New York City) is going down the drain immediately.

Specific groups such as paratroopers, the Green Berets and the Eagle Scouts have purposefully altered a regulation uniform in order both to stand out in a crowd and to portray an image of bravery or risk-taking. Some nurses have done the same thing. The stethoscope draped around the neck of the ICU nurse, and the O.R. scrub dress are two examples of purposeful alteration.

Stereotypes of appearance and what it signifies are common. Do you recognize these —

- Black suit, black shirt, white tie, slouch hat and heavy beard (the gangster)
- Navy or dark pinstripe suit, wing-tip shoes, white shirt, foulard silk tie (business executive, lawyer, broker)
- High heeled boots, denim jeans, broad brimmed white hat, plaid shirt, mackinaw (cowboy)
- Shirt cut to the navel, tight leather pants, long hair, sequinned vest (punk rock)
- Black dress, black shoes and stockings, black head scarf, no makeup (Mediterranean matron)

There are many, many more images that are immediately established by appearance or dress; the religious, the artist, the "hooker," the absent-minded professor, the radical, the model, and the nurse. What people wear and how they look does convey an impression. What you see may not be what you get, but it is what you expect, at least initially.

Response to Appearance and Image

Why can't I look the way I want? Isn't it insincere and hypocritical to dress purposely in a way that conveys an "image?" These are reasonable questions. However, the fact is that people do respond to image and appearance.

Several years ago, researchers studied the response of landlords to prospective tenants who were either obese or of average weight. Those of average weight and body size had significantly greater success in renting apartments than did the obese applicants. Another example — in a recent television movie, Sidney Poitier demonstrates to unemployed black youths the success of one of them when he changes his appearance and verbal approach to conform with middle class values. We are all familiar with the example of the undercover agents who, in order to infiltrate the criminal world, wear the dress of the people they hope eventually to apprehend.

Ultimately, effectiveness and ability will be demonstrated by behavior and job performance. But in the meantime even Cinderella knew better than to go to the ball in her rags. To get a prince, or at least to attract his attention, you need to look like a princess!

INVESTING IN YOUR IMAGE AND APPEARANCE

When to Buy, Where To Buy, How Much to Spend

There is no specific rule of thumb to determine how to much to spend yearly on new clothes. How much is spent depends on what is already in your wardrobe, what other financial commitments you may have, and how variable your wardrobe needs to be. The nurse executive or consultant will need a more varied professional wardrobe than the nurse who is in clinical practice.

Generally, however, it is a better investment to buy a few quality garments than a great many inexpensive items. This is especially true for garments that you expect to wear often and for several seasons, such as a winter coat or a raincoat. Shoes also fall into this category; better a few pairs of high quality than many cheap pairs. Money can be saved by taking advantage of end-of-the-season sales and closeouts. The risk in doing this, however, is that styles may be very different the following year.

Purchases in outlet or wholesale houses may also save money and be a good investment. However, these stores generally have a cash only, no return policy. You also need to be willing and able to spend a lot of time shopping these places, since their stock changes frequently and includes a lot of trash. You need to recognize good fabrics and style and brands even when the label is absent. Name brands and designer labels can be found in every price range. Simply because a garment carries a brand name or designer label does not guarantee good quality of workmanship. However, you can count on consistency in fit, style, or a "look." Find a brand or designer that suits your taste, your pocketbook, and your figure. You can then depend on garments from that label or designer fitting into the rest of your wardrobe. Look for sales of your favorite brand or designer label, since you know what you will be getting and that it will fit. Sizing can vary greatly among makers, so having a favorite brand also ensures a good fit. Don't buy because of the brand name or designer, but because of the match between your needs and the product. A designer dress at half-price that doesn't fit or is unbecoming is no bargain.

Try to anticipate what you may have to spend by making a plan for each season or year. Make a list of what you have that is becoming, in style and wearable. Then identify what you need to fill in the gaps. Try to coordinate your wardrobe so that garments can be worn as parts of several outfits. Avoid a great variety of fabrics and colors that will require additional handbags and shoes. Solid colors are usually more versatile as they can be mixed together, or matched with tweeds, plaids, and subtle patterns.

Some Common Misconceptions

Wash and wear fabrics are more desirable because of their easy care.
It is true that it is more costly to dry clean garments than it is to hand or machine wash — but dry cleaning looks better. Dry cleaning gives a more finished, professional, and expensive look to fabrics. Washable fabrics make sense for items that you wear frequently and that you intend to replace each season — such as blouses. If you do wash make sure you press the garment before wearing unless you like looking drip-dried! Natural fabric clothes — wool, cotton, linen, silk and blends — are much better long term investments even though they require professional dry cleaning. Natural fabrics look better, feel better and last longer. A practical basic winter wardrobe can begin with a three piece wool suit, several washable sweaters and blouses, a few silk scarves, a second pair of tailored trousers, a second skirt and a silk shirtdress.

"Dirt colors" are good because they don't show soiling.   These colors are generally drab and ugly. Some common "dirt colors" are mustardy gold, yuck green, and murky blue. They don't show the dirt but they don't do anything for your appearance either. Clear primary colors are much more becoming. Beige, black, true reds, dark brown, navy blue, and white are always in fashion and generally look well on everyone. Trying to match or mix colors can be hazardous unless you have a good color sense. Black and white, however, complement almost every other color.

Style and Fashion

How do you know what is in fashion? Fashion and style are not necessarily the same. Designers often try to be trend setters or to capture a larger share of the market by creating a high fashion line. Only the very rich, the very young, the very thin, or the very beautiful can wear these high fashion outfits. Remember the sack, the mini, and the "new look" — all highstyle but fashion disasters. Most women are better off modifying classic styles to conform with the latest fashion. Adjusting hemlines, jacket lengths, waist lines, and shoulder pads can do a great deal to change a fashion look. It may be fun to have one or two trendy items in a wardrobe, but it is generally not a good longterm investment. There are several styles that never go out of fashion — straight leg trousers, the one-piece maillot, the long-sleeved shirtwaist dress, the Chanel suit, and the cardigan sweater. These are simple designs that look well on almost everyone. The smart woman has a distinctive look that complements her and is in touch with the current look or style.

What About Makeovers?

Appearance doesn't end with clothes. Make-up, hair style and posture are also part of your image. It is very easy to become "accustomed to her face." We look in the mirror and see a familiar look — a look that may be comfortable and attractive, but out-of-date, or incongruent with the changes that go with aging. Color and texture of both hair and skin change as we grow older. A makeup and hairstyle that was suitable in a twenty year old girl is usually not attractive on a forty or fifty year old woman. Also, there is absolutely nothing like a new hairstyle or makeup change to boost the ego.

There are numerous salons and shops which provide a complete hair and cosmetic make-over. All of these make-overs cost money and time. There is the cost both of the initial visit and of the supply of cosmetics. There is usually a maintenance or upkeep cost also (sounds like buying a condominium!).

As with clothes, it is better to invest in a becoming hair and makeup style than in what is trendy. Hair does grow out, but it can be agonizing while you're waiting for it to get back to the color, length, or shape you want. If you want to experiment with a color change, use one of the rinse out tints first.

Expensive cosmetics are probably no better than moderately priced brands that look just as good and can be discarded without guilt feelings. Again, moderation is better than going overboard. Save the gilded eyelids and purple nail polish for Saturday nite out-of-town.

Even the most tasteful, attractive and stylish outfit can be spoiled by poor posture or careless deportment. Slumped shoulders, slack abdomen, and a sunken chest gives an "I don't care," or "I don't have any self-confidence" look. The West Point posture goes to the other extreme and is too stiff. A desirable standing posture is a compromise between the debutante slouch and "at-attention." The posture used for sitting is also important. The back should be straight with both feet on the floor or legs crossed at the ankle. Knees should be together at all times, even when wearing trousers. (Unless, of course, you are having a business lunch in a traditional Japanese restaurant where the Lotus position is expected.)

There is considerable interest and emphasis today on physical fitness and weight control. Opportunities abound for becoming trim and fit. Health spas, dance classes, exercise routines, fat-farms and diets by the hundreds are all in vogue. By careful consideration of the costs and benefits of these programs you can select which one, if any, is right for you. Many are expensive in time, dollars and energy with little guaranteed return. As with other fashions, avoid trends and slavish adherence.

A FINAL WORD

All of the foregoing advice is intended to be considered in the context of your professional and business role where the values, customs and expectations of others need to be considered in decisions about appearance. Women who have been successful know this and comply with those old truisms — "When in Rome, do as the Romans" — and "one picture is worth ten thousand words."

8 Investing in Education

Dorothy J. del Bueno

EDUCATION IS an investment in human resources. Theoretically, the payoffs or benefits from educational investment are of value both to the specific individual and to society at large. The classic economic test of the worth of an investment is the relationship between the allocation of resources and the stream of earnings — or — to put it in simple terms, do the benefits equal or exceed the costs? Unlike the other investments described in subsequent chapters of this book, education is a subjective investment. It is difficult to measure objectively the outcomes or benefits derived from education. Even the costs cannot be totally measured in dollars and cents. Therefore, each reader will need to consider personal values and circumstances in considering education as an investment.

WHY INVEST IN EDUCATION?

There are several reasons for investing in additional education. The most obvious and material of these is to increase present or future earnings. Although it seems logical to assume that more education will translate into more money, this is not necessarily true.

A great many studies have been done in both the business sector and in the professions to determine the economic return on education. Although the results are often ambiguous and contradictory, generally education does not have a high correlation with increased earnings or at least an increase that is sufficiently great to offset the costs. It is true, of course, that certain professions such as medicine that require advanced degrees do average a very high income level. This is not necessarily true, however, in other professions such as architecture and engineering. Contrarily, many top executives earning enormous salaries have no advanced degrees beyond a baccalaureate. Often the top earners in our society, entertainers and sports stars, have very little education beyond secondary school.

In nursing, earnings often depend on what level job you are currently in or will be able to obtain. At the staff nurse level, many hospitals or employing agencies do not pay extra for baccalaureate or graduate education. Even if there is an education differential it is not of sufficient magnitude to offset the costs in dollars and time needed to obtain the degree. Graduate degrees in nursing — masters and doctorates — may warrant larger salaries depending on whether or not the degree is a requirement for entry into the job. For example, in most schools of nursing a masters degree is a minimum requirement, the salary is at entry level and is low. In the service setting a masters degree may be required for a staff development or clinical specialist job, but the salary is several steps above the entry level salary for nurses in general and is considerably higher than the academic salary. It is somewhat ironic that the baccalaureate degree, often the most costly to obtain, especially for the diploma graduate, has the lowest economic payoff. The masters degree is often obtained with financial aid in scholarships and grants, takes a shorter period of time, and often yields a greater financial benefit. A graduate degree must be built on a baccalaureate however, and the costs of both should be combined to determine the actual monetary cost/benefit ratio.

There are a few top jobs in nursing, generally administrative positions, that pay salaries in the $50,000.00 to $100,000.00 range. These jobs do require advanced education and are therefore out of the reach of someone without it. In general however, a nurse can expect to earn a great deal of money only as an entrepreneur, or as one who assumes the risk and management of a business enterprise. Chapters 3 through 6 discuss the nurse as an entrepreneur.

If increased salary is not the best reason for investing in education, what are the other reasons? An economic reality in some instances is that advanced degrees may be mandated to keep your job. Academic institutions often require a doctorate to stay in the position or to allow entry into the tenure track. A number of hospitals are now requiring a baccalaureate degree or masters degree for any position above staff nurse. Continuing education is mandatory in a number of states to renew an active license, a requirement for working as a nurse. Also, nurses who have been out of nursing may be required to take a refresher course prior to obtaining employment. In these cases education is a necessary investment simply to maintain present earnings.

Another reason to invest in education is for the benefit of contacts. It has often been said, somewhat cynically, that rich people (and the not-so-rich) send their children to private school in order to make important contacts that will have later payoffs. In the days before women's liberation, many a young women was sent to a "finishing" school or women's college in order to meet a future husband (a rich one was the ideal, of course!) in another school nearby. A degree from Harvard, Yale, or Wharton is valuable per se, but is also valuable for the contacts it carries and for the "old-boy" network associated with such an experience.

Unless the education experience is totally external or independent in nature, it provides the opportunity for meeting people who can be presently or potentially helpful. The old saying — "it's not what you know, but who you know that counts" is a reality. Knowing people in influential positions or with expert knowledge and experience can be very valuable. Once you become known to or part of an inner circle, the opportunities for better positions become more numerous. Having contacts is also very important to the nurse who may wish later to become an entrepreneur. Always remember, however, once you are "in" to help others who are in the same position you once were — become a contact for other nurses.

Education often is a legitimate excuse for leaving an undesirable job. Many organizations provide sabbaticals or educational leaves-of-absence for employees. A leave provides some job security while also allowing an opportunity to seek other work while getting the education. Most employers who give educational leaves guarantee some position in the agency on return. Often, even if the educational leave was a desperation strategy, it turns out to be a positive experience and helps you to acquire a new perspective.

Many people invest in education not for economic reasons, but for the self-satisfaction and pleasure they derive from education itself. An educational experience has the potential for opening new intellectual and philosophical horizons. There can be great pleasure in associating with others in a learning experience if only for the socialization. Learning can be exciting and satisfying. It can be a way to escape from the day-to-day stress and crisis orientation of many jobs. Learning can refresh the mind and the spirit, benefits that cannot be measured in dollars and cents.

WHAT KIND OF EDUCATIONAL INVESTMENT SHOULD YOU MAKE?

All education requires an investment of time, money, energy, or foregone earnings (money you would be earning if you weren't going to school). Therefore, it is important from an economic perspective to choose the right kind of education. The article from *R.N. Magazine* reprinted at the end of this chapter describes a method for choosing a nursing baccalaureate. But on what basis do you choose between a nursing or non-nursing degree? The primary factor should be "what you want to be when you grow up." If you are sure that you will always be practicing or teaching nursing, then degrees in nursing are an absolute necessity. If you see yourself in administrative or entrepreneurial positions, then degrees in other disciplines may be more appropriate. Degrees in business, law, administration, public policy or political science may be more relevant if your future is in government, public health, or industry. The content as well as the contacts acquired in these educational experiences may prove to be necessary and valuable. Of course, you could obtain double degrees in nursing and other disciplines or professions. The additional dollar and time costs of this option may be prohibitive, however.

Availability is another variable to consider. The opportunities for education in your location may be limited. Unless you are able to change locations, you may have to settle for what is there, or hope that additional programs will become available. Whether you choose nursing or non-nursing degrees be sure to consider the following before investing your time, money, and energy: reputation of the school or program, dollar investment required, time investment required, flexibility in scheduling, and the relevance of the curriculum to your goals and objectives.

An alternative to degree-granting education is continuing education or adult extension education that awards certificates of attendance or continuing education credits. Generally, the chief advantages of this kind of education are: lower cost, less time, and greater availability. Many nurse practitioners have been educated in certificate programs that were six to nine months in length. These practitioners are functioning competently and making a considerable contribution to health care. Many programs in administration are non-degree granting but are considered to be of top quality. The primary disadvantage of the non-degree educational programs is the future acceptance of employers or academic institutions even though the content and quality may have been equal to or even superior to that in a degree program. In a market where supply of potential employees is greater than actual jobs there will be more rigid requirements for formal degree prepared people. Also, non-degree education is generally not accepted as meeting entry requirements for advanced degrees. Therefore, additional time will have to be spent on obtaining the necessary credits prior to entry into the graduate degree program.

There are short-term non-credit courses that can have definite economic payoff. Courses in proposal writing, grant writing, and creative writing are especially beneficial for academics and consultants. Effective writing skills will improve your ability to get published, to have proposals and grants funded, and to let the world know of your particular expert knowledge. Courses in public speaking or platform skills are almost a prerequisite for the professional lecturer who is not naturally talented. Courses in persuasion and selling techniques can reap benefits for almost anyone who has to influence others in the context of their job. As described in Chapter 7, "Image and Appearance," investment in courses that improve your "presentation of self" is almost sure to pay off in real benefits.

Whether your educational investment is in degree programs, continuing professional education, or self-help courses, it is important to know what you want to accomplish, or your objectives, and why you want it, or your motivation. Once your motives and objectives are clear, then shop around and choose the best educational buy you can find. When you invest in education you invest in yourself and your future — so make the investment a thoughtful and purposeful one.

IN SEARCH OF THE BSN

How to find a reputable school with sane requirements

It's not easy, but it can be done.   Until recently, it didn't much matter whether you wanted a BSN or not, because programs for working RNs were so scarce that only the fanatically dedicated could gain admission and stick it out. Now, that dismal picture is beginning to change.

A recent *RN* poll of the 50 states, the Virgin Islands, and Puerto Rico indicates that every state and territory has some plans to increase educational opportunities for RNs. Some are farther along than others, but a substantial number of baccalaureate programs for licensed nurses already exist. More are becoming available all the time, too, as schools start new programs and revise existing ones to better accommodate licensed RNs.

So, how do you choose among them? To begin with, be sure to zero in on those that grant baccalaureate degrees **in nursing** — either a BSN or a BS with a major in nursing — because that's what you'll need if you want to get anywhere in the profession (see following article). Then, among the schools that meet this criterion, begin checking out those that look feasible in terms of two other fundamental factors: location and money.

Ask yourself how far you can — and are willing to — go in search of a baccalaureate degree. Can you relocate or manage a long commute? If not, you're limited to schools in your immediate area. If you *can* move, and you're interested in a school in another state, be sure to check the admission requirements. Some schools require that you hold a current nursing license in the state in which they're located. Also, remember that at most state universities, fees for out-of-state students are considerably higher than for state residents, and that there may be fairly stringent limits on the number of out-of-state students admitted.

Beyond location, there's the ever-vexing question of finances. Do you have money put aside? Can you afford to stop working or to work part time? If not, your choices are narrowed even further. Many, though by no means all, BSN programs require at least some full-time attendance. And, though most schools do have some form of financial aid available, it may be only for full-time students, and probably won't make up for a complete loss of income. So, if your budget mandates that you work, concentrate your search on programs that allow you to complete your degree mostly or entirely on a part-time basis.

When in doubt, ask

Your next step is to start collecting information. Choose a few schools within your geographical limits, ones with BSN programs that admit RNs, and write to them for catalogues and admission forms. The directory beginning on page 64 should give you a start. The National League for Nursing's list of all NLN-accredited nursing baccalaureate programs in the United States can help as well.

Review the catalogue information, write down any questions you have, and, if possible, make an appointment to speak with the dean of nursing or a faculty member in the RN program. Don't be afraid to ask about anything you don't understand. Catalogues can be confusing, and you'll need to understand program requirements thoroughly to make an intelligent decision.

Try also to talk to other nurses who are enrolled in, or have graduated from, the programs that interest you. Have them describe their educational needs and experiences. What do they like? What do they dislike? Do they feel their program has met their needs? If not, why not? Remember, however, that their needs may be different from your own.

This kind of feedback can help you decide whether a program lives up to its paper promises. For example, some schools that *accept* RNs don't really *welcome* them or go out of their way to accommodate them, while others are extremely responsive to their needs. And there are always a few programs that, to put it bluntly, are rip-offs. In many cases, the people best able to tell you these things are the students or ex-students.

Some key questions

Here are the key ones to keep in mind when you begin your enquiries:

Is the program accredited by the National League for Nursing (or is it in the process of accreditation)? Although sound programs exist that haven't sought NLN accreditation, which is voluntary, accreditation does insure that a program meets certain educational standards. Furthermore, graduation from an NLN-accredited undergraduate program is a criterion for admission to many graduate programs in nursing. You may have no intention of going to graduate school, but it's always smart to be prepared in case you change your mind. Don't forget, too, that most financial assistance from government funding sources is contingent on attendance at an NLN-accredited school.

The catch here is that many programs — especially those designed specifically for RNs — are so new that they haven't yet had a chance to apply for accreditation (a program isn't eligible until it graduates its first class). If you're interested in one of these, ask whether the school has applied, or intends to apply, for accreditation, and take an extra close look at the program itself to make sure it's viable.

What type of program is it? Some schools with "generic" BSN programs (those preparing students for licensure) admit already-licensed nurses with advanced standing. Others have specially tailored programs for RNs only. Still others take an integrated career ladder approach or award degrees based entirely on assessment of learning. Each type has its own advantages and disadvantages, depending on your needs. (For more on the different types, see the following article.)

Can you transfer or challenge credits? To get a baccalaureate degree, you generally have to accumulate 120 or more academic credits. Obviously, the fewer courses you have to take to get those credits, the more time and money you'll save. Therefore, it's very important to find out how many and which of the required credits you'll have to earn through course work and how many you can transfer or challenge based on previous learning and experience.

"Transfer" means that the school will recognize and award credit for courses you've taken at another academic institution, usually a two-year or four-year college. This is **not** the same thing as the automatic, or blanket, credit given by some schools for prior education or life experience. Most schools award transfer credit on a course-by-course basis, and the number of credits you receive depends on an evaluation of transcript records, course descriptions, and/or catalogue descriptions. *Credits from a diploma school generally won't transfer,* or won't transfer as readily as credits from associate degree programs (or other baccalaureate programs).

"Challenge" means taking an examination on the content of a course. If you pass, you receive credit for that course without taking it. Schools may also use examinations to determine advanced placement in an academic program. For example, passing a placement or proficiency examination may exempt you from all or most junior-level courses.

Challenge exams come in several varieties. They may be standardized tests, such as those given through the College Level Examination Program (CLEP), the American College Testing Program (ACT), and the National League for Nursing, or they may be "teacher-made" tests developed by college faculty for specific courses and subject areas. Most challenge exams test knowledge, but some schools also give tests that assess clinical performance.

Transfer and challenge policies vary from school to school. For example, some schools allow transfer and challenge of both nursing and non-nursing credits. Others transfer only non-nursing credits, but allow you to challenge both nursing and non-nursing courses. Many schools also set specific limits on the number of credits you can transfer or challenge. Make sure you thoroughly understand the rules before you apply.

Another interesting wrinkle in the challenge system has been developed by a few schools, like the University of Alabama, which allow RN students to "validate" lower level (junior year) nursing courses by successfully completing upper level (senior year) courses. Upon successful completion of specified upper level courses, you receive credit for certain lower level courses without actually having to take them.

How flexible is the program? In other words, will the courses you do have to take be available when you're free? This, too, varies greatly from program to program. More and more schools are instituting at least some weekend, evening, and/or late afternoon classes for RNs who work during the day. And some actually offer **all** required courses on weekends and evenings. For example, the University of North Carolina at Charlotte repeats daytime classes in the evening, and C.W. Post College, Greenvale, New York, allows nurses to complete their degrees through an all-weekend program.

Some programs are self-paced and can be completed off site (that is, without attending classes at a main campus). For example, New York State's external degree program (see following article) requires no on-campus study. Other schools, such as the Medical University of South Carolina, conduct programs on so-called satellite campuses in a different part of the state, or another state altogether (MUSC's satellite campus is Winthrop College in North

Which Program 'Wins'?

Here's a chance to flex your decision-making muscles on a couple of mythical baccalaureate programs before you tackle the real thing. First, rank all the factors discussed in the accompanying article according to their importance to **you** (assign Number 1 to the factor that's **most** important). Then compare the program descriptions below and, for each factor, award **your** rank number to the program that best meets your needs. Add up each program's collection of rank numbers to get its "score." The program with the lower score "wins."

Try using a similar system on the real programs you're considering. It may bring things into focus.

Factor	Your Ranking	Program A	Program B	"Winning" Program insert rank number of this factor next to the better program	
				A	B
Cost		Expensive (more than $5,000 to complete). No scholarships	Reasonable (less than $5,000 to complete). No scholarships		
Location		Convenient— within commuting distance	Convenient— within commuting distance		
Non-Accredited?		Yes	Yes		
Type Of Program		Generic BSN with advanced standing and some courses designed for RNs	RN/BSN (RNs only) program separate from generic program		

Full-Time	None	One semester must be taken full time
Transfer Credits	Non-nursing courses only, maximum of 60 credits	Non-nursing courses only, maximum of 45 credits
Challenge Credits	All non-nursing courses and nursing courses, except for fourth-year courses	Non-nursing maximum of 45 credits, including transfer credit. Nursing courses: only first four courses
Flexibility	Most required non-nursing courses given during daytime hours. Nursing courses given during the day, Monday to Friday	Required non-nursing courses given days, with some evening classes available. Nursing theory courses given during the day; clinical hours arranged individually
Reputation	Established, program	Relatively new. Graduated one class from RN program. Positive comments from students

Factor	Your Ranking	Program A	Program B	"Winning" Program insert rank number of this factor next to the better program	
				A	B
Program Goals		Same as for generic students	Same as for generic students		
Faculty		All have minimum of master's degree. ratio of 1:15. Faculty teach in both generic and RN programs	All have minimum of master's degree. ratio of 1:10. Faculty teach in RN program only		
Graduate Program?		Yes	No		

Carolina). And in several states, including Michigan, Wisconsin, and Montana, there are outreach programs in which faculty from various baccalaureate nursing schools give courses at off-campus locations.

Although flexibility is still a problem in many places, growing numbers of schools are revising their programs to better accommodate working RNs. Be on the lookout for an increase in programs that stress flexibility. But, if you plan to complete your degree entirely part time, be sure to ask whether the school has a deadline for completion.

What kind of reputation or image does the school and program have? Has anyone in your community or hospital ever heard of it? What have they heard? Do students and graduates of the program speak positively about their experiences? It's especially important to ask these questions about unaccredited programs, but you should check out accredited ones, too. Accreditation doesn't automatically guarantee satisfaction.

Find out how old the program is. A new program without an established reputation may be sound and innovative, but it could also have implementation problems — in other words, they're still getting the bugs out. On the other hand, an older program, no matter how reputable, may be less flexible and responsive to your needs.

If the program is new, ask whether it's "experimental" or a pilot project. Such programs often rely on external funding from grants and other sources, and they sometimes disappear when the outside funds run out.

If the program is for RNs only, are its overall objectives of the same quality as those of generic programs? Your baccalaureate degree as an RN should meet standards just as stringent as those for a generic degree. It's perfectly all right for a so-called RN/BSN or BRN program to be separate from a generic program and provide different learning experiences, but it shouldn't be a watered-down version of the generic program. RNs aren't second-class students.

Are qualified faculty members available for consultation and supervision? Availability, more than numbers, is the key here. For example, do faculty members have established office hours or on-call hours for students? While there's no standard faculty-student ratio for a BSN program, the teaching staff should be large enough to provide adequate supervision while you're learning new skills, and to give you help if you're having trouble meeting learning objectives. Nursing Department faculty who also teach in other programs at the school should always have enough time available to meet the needs of their nursing students. As for academic credentials, faculty members in a baccalaureate program should hold masters or doctoral degrees.

Finally, does the school have a graduate program in nursing? This question probably isn't as crucial to you as some of the others. However, if you do expect to go on to graduate work, it's generally easier to matriculate into the graduate program at the same school you did your undergraduate work in. Also, a school with a graduate program may have more faculty with research experience and doctoral degrees — all of which can be an additional educational resource for you.

The baccalaureate program that meets all your criteria, and is nevertheless affordable and conveniently located, is your ideal program — and it probably doesn't exist. Trade-offs and compromises are therefore in order. You'll have to decide which criteria are most important to you personally, and be satisfied with a school that at least meets those minimum requirements.

Whatever program you finally choose, expect some disappointments. No program is perfect. Some of your experiences will, with any luck, be exhilarating. Others may be dull or repetitive. But one thing is certain — you'll never be the same person, or nurse, again. You may not believe it now, but your investment in yourself will be a good one. Take it from one who has been there. Good luck.

9 Getting Published

Christopher Campbell

WHY PUBLISH?

THE MOTIVES for nurses' publishing can be as diverse as those for pursuing higher educational degrees or higher levels of clinical expertise. To a far greater extent than other groups nurses are generally motivated to write by altruism. Nurses want to help their professional colleagues deliver better service and quality patient care. Such labors of love have indeed contributed significantly to the quality of life in our society. Any profit derived from professional writing is therefore generally satisfaction, and may not be matched by profits of the more literal, tangible sort required for successful commercial publishing. Therein lies a real, practical problem for the would-be author.

Nurses may also decide to write for other reasons, such as the indirect benefits of increased visibility, recognition and prestige. These are perfectly legitimate ends that can be attained without compromising the more altruistic motivations. If such benefits run counter to the basic laws of economics, compromise with the profit motive may become an inescapable fact. A nurse author to be forearmed, should be forewarned about what to expect in the capitalistic business world.

Publishing **is** a business. It is a relatively enlightened one, but a business nonetheless. Like all businesses it must turn at least a modest profit to remain alive and well. Consequently, publishers are happiest with publications that pay their own way in the marketplace, and with authors who find it natural and reasonable to earn money from their writing.

WHAT TO PUBLISH

Before investing a lot of time, energy and money in the preparation of a manuscript it is only sensible to make sure that your proposed publication fits a publisher's needs. What is **likely** to be accepted by a publisher is ultimately determined by economics. Therefore, as in all other sectors of the economy, attention must be given to the laws of supply and demand.

What you as an author can **supply** is the nursing knowledge you know best and, more specifically, know better than your colleagues. This is a **pre**-condition to successful writing. Developing a manuscript as a heuristic exercise, in order to organize and analyze your own thoughts, is **not** a good approach. This is particularly true if you have led a publisher to believe that you are already well versed in your topic, in which case it is also unethical. On the other hand, if you do know your subject well and are confident that you can present it better than others have, the fact that you have not written previously should not be a deterrent. No one is born knowing how to create perfect prose. There are very few authors to whom writing comes effortlessly. Veteran writer Gene Fowler said that "writing is easy; all you do is sit staring at the blank sheet of paper until the drops of blood form on your forehead[9]."

If you can communicate your subject matter at all — verbally, as in the classroom, or by demonstration, as in clinical practice — then changing to the medium of the written word is not an insurmountable obstacle. The first necessary step is to make an objective appraisal of your delivery or style. Identify exactly what it is that you do differently from and more successfully than others. For instance, if you use analogy and metaphor to good effect in conveying difficult concepts, these techniques can be translated directly into writing. If you have a knack for reducing complex procedures into series of easy-to-follow steps, you already have the beginnings of a handbook or outline-style text. If you use charts and diagrams as a takeoff point for complicated explanations you may use such graphic techniques to develop a written narrative. Case histories used as a means of illustrating real life situations also can be recreated vividly in prose. The most important points are to recognize your strengths, the things that come to you naturally, and allow your prose to reflect them. Attempting to adapt your natural style to some preconceived notion of proper prose is undesirable as it inevitably leads to a forced, artificial narrative useful only as a cure for readers with insomnia. Tell what you know best in a comfortable personal style.

A good publisher will help you determine what the marketplace needs and to tailor your publication accordingly. You, of course, can save yourself a good deal of unnecessary work, and enhance the chances of quick acceptance of your proposal, by conducting a preliminary market survey of your own. First of all, be sure that what you propose to write has not in fact been written before. More and more publishers have been attracted to the vast nursing market, often emphasizing sales over editorial depth. Attempts to improve on existing publications have most often resulted in duplications, with little or no net advantage to the reader, the writer or the publisher. A surprising number of proposals, and sometimes finished manuscripts, come across editors' desks without their authors' first having searched the literature sufficiently to realize that they are "reinventing the wheel." This does not preclude the **repackaging** of existing knowledge in some more useful format, which, to one degree or another, is the essence of most professional publishing. Presenting worthwhile material better and more effectively than previous authors is simply a better matching of supply to demand. The improvement, however, must be genuine and thorough enough to create a new product. Saturation of the market with essentially cloned publications ultimately has little worth to anyone.

The next aspect of matching supply to demand, and perhaps the most frequently overlooked and underemphasized, is to identify precisely the target audience. The target audience is the one for whom the manuscript is developed and written. Many authors mistakenly believe that everyone else will be as interested in their work as they are themselves, a rather naive opinion rarely borne out by subsequent sales figures. Even more unfortunate is the fact that many publishers, despite their supposedly greater objectivity, also get carried away by an initial flush of optimism. This is especially so when the publisher is represented by a junior editor under great pressure to "produce" books.

What are the basic facts of demand? First, as used here, "demand" refers to the specific needs of specific nurses practicing in specific professional environments. A publication that attempts to meet the **different** needs of **different** groups of nurses will be only partially useful to any of them. Consumers are quite logically disinclined to pay for any book or journal of which they will use only a fraction. At the other extreme, a publication that tries to limit itself to only universally relevant material risks being so superficial as to be totally expendable. Anything in the nursing world that is "good for all of the people all of the time" will certainly have been done before.

An exact definition of the readership for a publication may indicate an audience too small to justify the publisher's investment, or too scattered to reach economically. These points emphasize the fundamental rule that, regardless of the size and nature of the market, there is always a *cost* attached to reaching potential consumers. These costs must be covered by the price of the publication. In the case of a widely scattered readership it might become prohibitively expensive to advertise indiscriminately to vast numbers of non-buyers in order to reach the relatively few buyers who must then pay for the entire advertising expense. Conversely, the audience may be well defined and of manageable size, but difficult to reach. For example there are enough nurses taking continuing education courses in the management of drug addiction to make a book on this topic profitable. Unfortunately, publishers have no sure means of knowing where and when these courses are given in order to single about the prospective buyers in advance. Finally, to assure a sufficiently large audience for an intended publication, avoid the common trap of assuming that what is useful in your particular professional setting will be equally applicable elsewhere. Material of commercial potential must be specific enough to be put into practice by the reader, but not so specific to the author's environment that readers have to change their own settings in order to use it. For example, the respiratory ward in a major hospital may have an excellent procedures manual worthy of publication, but if it directs the user to report all incidents of a given sort to Mrs. Smith, or to use specific chart forms or supplies, the manual will be of local reference value only.

In summary, for a publication to be a worthwhile investment from anyone's point of view; it must be original, have a discreet, large and accessible audience, and be presented in a practical, relevant format. To write something that meets all of these criteria is usually quite a lot of work. It is obviously to the writer's advantage, therefore, to be certain that the criteria have been met **before** going in search of a publisher.

WHERE TO PUBLISH

What sort of publisher should you search for? In tailoring content to a specific audience, the medium in which you publish is one of the first choices you will have to make. In nursing the media are largely restricted to journals, books and audio-visuals. Although deciding which of these is best suited to your work is normally not difficult, there are some basic guidelines that will help you.

Writing for Journals

Professional periodicals or journals are distinguished by the relative brevity of published articles, the frequency of publication, the currency of the information they contain, and their well-defined readership. Manuscripts of less than book length and of a "newsy" nature therefore have good potential for journals. Articles describing current clinical and educational practices based on common background concepts or knowledge are also suitable for journals. A related series of articles on a complex subject also can be published in a journal series.

What subject matter is appropriate for which journals, and vice versa, is usually quite evident. There are however some subtle but significant differences. Some nursing magazines are the official organs of formally constituted groups within the profession. These journals are partially supported by dues rather than directly through subscriptions. Other journals are popular publications, supported solely by advertising and subscriptions. Other journals are "refereed," meaning that articles are reviewed by peers prior to acceptance rather than accepted or rejected by journal editors. Although refereed journals are generally considered to be rather more prestigious than non-refereed, the fate of articles submitted to them depends to a great extent on luck as there is no guarantee that all referees have the same high level of expertise, or editorial skills. Conversely, a board of professional editors is much more likely to judge the literary quality of articles accurately and consistently, but may not have expert knowledge of nursing content. The reputation of a long-standing journal among your own peers is generally a good guide.

Another notable difference in journals is that some will pay you for the privilege of publishing your article while others, by expecting you to bear the expenses of manuscript preparation, in effect let you pay **them** for the privilege of gracing their pages. The pay/no pay variable has some effect on the number of manuscripts submitted, and the number consequently refused. One thing remains constant: publishing in journals is the easiest and quickest route to professional visibility and recognition. Any journal with a decent reputation is therefore going to receive more proposals for articles than it can actually publish.

There are a few things you can do to increase the probability of being published. First, do not submit inappropriate material. Sending an esoteric research report to one of the more popular journals is a waste of time and postage. Second, consult and follow the ground rules laid down by each journal. Some insist on seeing abstracts prior to finished manuscript, most have length restrictions, and all have style guidelines. All of this information usually appears on the pages containing the table of contents or "masthead." If not included there, the guidelines will be sent on request.

Finally, there is the touchy question of multiple submissions. Some journals specifically require that they receive an exclusive opportunity to consider an article, but they may also require six months to a year to reach a decision. It is only fair to yourself to make use of the leverage that competition among publishers gives. In return, it is only ethical to be candid. Let each journal know if you have submitted the manuscript to other journals. This will tend to hasten decision making on acceptance or rejection. As soon as you receive acceptance for publication by one journal, inform the others immediately so that they do not invest additional editorial time and money.

Writing A Book

The decision to write a book obviously cannot be made as casually as the decision to write an article, but the differences are more quantitative than qualitative. To write a book normally takes a broader knowledge base, more time, more informational and clerical resources and, frequently, more help in the form of co-authors or contributors. Considering the magnitude of such an investment it is only prudent to wait until you have received a commitment from a publisher before investing too much in the project. A finished manuscript, even of high quality, may be rejected because it doesn't meet a publisher's physical requirements or some other seemingly arbitrary standard. Virtually all publishers issue guidelines for manuscript formats. While it is regrettably true that most of them do not think to share with authors the reasons behind some of these less-than-self-explanatory rules, reasons for them do exist. Failure to follow these specifications may make a manuscript too expensive for the publisher to manufacture at a reasonable cost. For example, the incorrect placement of arrows or labels on a photograph may make it unreproduceable. Or, the painstaking preparation of multi-page fold-out charts may be wasted if they are illegible when reduced to actual page size.*

So, make sure you play according to a mutually understood set of rules, that you have assessed the size of the undertaking carefully, and that you have the resources to complete it successfully. Bear in mind also that a book, unlike an article, is generally a comprehensive, self-contained unit, and is written with the aim and expectation that its contents will have enough enduring value to justify its publication in a relatively permanent form. Your publisher will be very conscious of this last requirement because a nursing book may have to sell for a year or more just to break even financially.

Writing For Other Media

A considerable amount of nursing content is published in the form of films, audio cassettes, visual teaching aids and related media. Some of these media presentations are done originally by the audio-visual departments of schools. To produce them for commercial distribution is simply a matter of identifying a competent manufacturer with adequate selling resources. However, many media productions are related to written publications of some kind. Since these other media may not even have been thought of at the time the written publications were planned, the selection of your book or journal publisher should be made with the possibility of such "spin-offs" taken into account. Suffice it to say that there are some nursing publishers that have multi-media divisions or related companies, and many more publishers that sub-contract this sort of

*The publisher of the present volume makes available upon request a concise set of manuscript preparation guidelines which are general enough to be widely applicable. The reasons for the given physical specifications are also explained.

production. In either case, authors need to be aware of copyright implications when approaching or selecting a particular publisher — which brings us to the important matter of . . .

CHOOSING, AND GETTING CHOSEN BY, A PUBLISHER

There are dozens of nursing publishers in the United States. The decision of which are worth approaching with your publishing idea requires some pre-sorting. The initial triage is not particularly difficult. If you have a sufficiently clear picture of what your publication is to be, it is by definition easy to identify those publishers that print the kind of publication you have in mind; For example, books versus articles, undergraduate texts versus high-level monographs, study guides versus reference books, procedure manuals versus programmed instruction.

The next step, less easy and more subjective, is singling out from this preselected group those publishers who are **best** at doing that kind of publication. You will have to rely chiefly on your own impressions and the opinions of your colleagues. Be sure, however, that your sampling of public opinion is broad enough to be statistically valid. A colleague whose perfectly awful manuscript has just been rejected by a particular company may think **them** awful when they have, in fact, done nothing more than make a sound business judgment. Also, consider how similar the companies' existing publications are to your own proposal. Even if you have heeded the warning not to reinvent the wheel, you ought to give some thought to whether your work will be complementary to, or potentially competitive with, their existing titles.

Advertising strength is another factor that should weigh heavily in your selection of a publishing house. Some publishers which primarily service the academic market still maintain large field sales staffs, while other publishers are turning increasingly to direct mail promotion. Publishers that specialize in relatively expensive monographs will tend towards equally specialized, "one-shot" ad campaigns, while those that publish across the nursing spectrum will usually tend towards a "scatter" approach, grouping a number of more or less related titles in each advertisement. Some publishers have direct sales capacities in the increasingly significant foreign markets, while others are represented overseas only through agents. The publisher presumably has well thought out reasons for its particular marketing strategies, and these should be shared with authors prior to contracting. The publisher, however, will not be able to come up with a finished advertising plan prior to contracting. Mutual communication about this important topic is, in itself, significant in evaluating your ability to work together smoothly.

Working together effectively is the most important (and most difficult to assess and predict) element in successful publishing. Editors are like midwives, and you have every right to be fussy about whom you allow to deliver your "baby." Again you may have to rely mostly on reputation. Find other authors an editor has collaborated with and ask them for references and opinions.

There are also more direct and concrete ways to evaluate the prospects for a good working relationship. First, find out what *kind* of editor you will work with (in the professional, not the psychoanalytic, sense).

Professionally, some editors are strictly responsible for "acquisitions," in which case you are going to be bounced along to some other editor as soon as the ink on your contract is dry. Others are "developmental editors" accustomed to working with the author in conceptualizing, organizing and writing the material. When both of these functions, acquisitions and development, are combined in one person the resulting title is usually just "Editor," although "Executive Editor," "Managing Editor" and other permutations occur. Regardless of titles, the ideal situation is that in which one editor is responsible for shepherding a manuscript from initial proposal to printed and promoted publication. This might be thought of as "primary editing." This editor should serve as your advocate and intermediary when dealing with the other publishing personnel who have a hand in the process: a copyeditor, who does most of the more routine editing and marking of directions for the printer on the manuscript proper; a production manager, who sees the text through the actual manufacturing process; and advertising people who handle different aspects of promotion. Consequently, the establishment of rapport with this editor and friend-in-court is really of the greatest significance, and worth determining in advance.

The editor's first responsibility is to be a sympathetic listener, and to assume that the publication you are proposing is worthwhile until and unless proven otherwise. Next, it helps if the editor demonstrates sufficient background or understanding of your field to permit a ready grasp of your intent. Knowledge of competing works is also an asset. It is fair to say, however, that editors who pretend to know **more** about your subject than you do are not going to be easy to work with. If they really know more they ought to be writing rather than editing. If they have a realistic perception of their own limitations they are more likely to remember that they are there to *serve* authors (who do, after all, pay the editors' salaries). On the other hand, the editor who is anxious to accept your project uncritically, who wants to offer a contract without having the proposal reviewed or without being able to describe it back to you, is similarly suspect. Either the editor personally or the publishing house collectively may be under pressure to come up with "product." To allow them to do so indiscriminately is to place your publication in poor company. Given the value of a good personal relationship with your editor, it is more than justified to test your judgment using the criteria described here before entering into a contractual obligation. Neither author nor editor will want this mating dance to drag on interminably, however. Usually, there is sufficient opportunity to make valid judgments from the editor's handling of your original proposal.

Presenting A Proposal

A large number of recent nursing books, especially the more lucrative ones, were actually conceived by editors who identified a need, used the professional "grapevine" for leads on good potential authors, and followed up until an agreement was reached with one or more authors. This reflects two factors; first, editors' access to better, fuller data on market needs and, second, a more intensive competition among the growing number of nursing publishers. Still, most of the best books originated with an author who had to sell the idea to a publisher. This is not always an easy task. If you are a first-time author you should be prepared for the fact that it *can* be as difficult as getting a first novel published. There are, however, some commonsense rules to follow which, if less than an absolute guarantee of success, will at least enhance the odds of your getting a fair chance.

It is a curious fact that a significant number of proposals a nursing editor receives "over the transom," or unsolicited, are from authors so modest that they provide no information beyond a title (or, perhaps, so immodest that they expect all the world to accept their ideas on faith). Such an approach, not surprisingly, starts things off on a rather negative note and discourages the editor from pursuing the project. The proposal with a clear, logical plan that evidences thoughtful consideration of factors already described, that contribute to the commercial and professional success of a publication, is much more likely to be received and reviewed with enthusiasm. For journal articles an abstract of the article's content is usually sufficient. For books a proposal needs to be more extensive and comprehensive.

Begin with a brief prose description of the planned project. Describe the kind of book you hope to write, such as a textbook, handbook or monograph. Outline your reasons for undertaking this project such as, the only other book like it is twenty years old and too difficult to consult as a ready reference, or there is nothing on the subject for undergraduates. Detail the objectives you expect the book will fulfill such as, assist nurses to pass the certification exam as pediatric nurse practitioners, or provide a comprehensive overview for faculty of conceptual frameworks. Identify in your proposal the specific audience intended. Stipulate what level and kinds of previous knowledge the reader will be expected to have before reading the book, such as college-level microbiology, a working command of common statistical procedures or calculus, clinical experience in emergency room care. Also define the level of proficiency that should be achieved after the book is read. If possible, estimate accurately and honestly the size of the intended audience. There is, for instance, a considerable difference between the total number of operating room nurses and the far smaller number of operating room supervisors; a relatively inexpensive book might be attractive for the former market while only a more expensive work would be profitable in the smaller one. Avoid suggesting ingenuously that your masterpiece-to-be will be "good for everyone." Such a statement means you have not analyzed the potential market at all or that you believe it will create its own market. With the possible exception of Yippie Abbie Hoffman's *Steal This Book* (which was reportedly shoplifted in record numbers), no book has ever literally created its own market. Sometimes the market is there, ready and waiting for the perfect book to come along and achieve an instant success but, again, demand is a **pre**-requisite to making supply profitable.

Although the prose description of the book will have outlined its scope in general terms, such as nursing care of respiratory disorders, include a complete and detailed table of contents. The details may, of course, be subject to later change. Editors realize that a manuscript always undergoes some further development as it takes shape, but the logic, clarity and practicability of your intended project should be demonstrated before either you or the editor feels ready to proceed.

The physical characteristics of your manuscript should be estimated as closely as possible before the fact. Project length in typed, double-spaced manuscript pages (which run a fairly consistent 250 words per page) rather than in printed pages, which can vary from 200 to 900 words per page depending on type-size, page-size, margin dimensions and number of columns. Estimate the number of illustrations as accurately as you can. These directly affect manufacturing costs and production time. The absolute need for color illustrations should always be specified clearly. Unfortunately, color illustrations are extremely costly and usually prohibitively so, except in mass markets.

Of prime interest to the editor is your own assessment of how your book will compete with other books. Modesty should not prevent you from pointing out the weak points in comparable publications, and vanity should not excuse you from defending the improvements you have made over these weaknesses. Inability to do both clearly and easily is a danger signal to both you and the editor. Another helpful hint on what **not** to say: Never dismiss the question of competition by claiming that your book has none. A book literally without competition is a book without a market. If there is a real need for such a product, people must be using *something,* and as one of these people you should be able to say what that is.

Present basic data about yourself in your first communication with the publisher. A *curriculum vitae* is not always necessary or always informative. You must establish your credentials as an authority on your topic and cite any related work that has helped prepare you for this project. An editor may or may not require a sample of your writing but, especially if you have not published previously, you might want to write a preliminary draft of a representative section in order to evaluate how quickly and easily you will progress.

Do include addresses and telephone numbers where you can be reached at different times and do take the time to prepare the proposal neatly. A letter filled with grammatical and typographical errors will naturally make a strong negative first impression. A photocopy of a photocopy or a fourth carbon may not be legible enough to make an impression of any kind. If you decide to submit a proposal to more than one publisher make sure that each is an original. Finally, don't enclose a stamped, self-addressed return envelope. Assuming that you are dealing only with publishers which can afford a first-class stamp, the return envelope all but shouts that you do not think yourself worth much of their time and that you expect to have your proposal rejected.

In summary, the factors that are likely to count in favor of your proposal are: quality, or how well organized and written your work is; and the three economic factors, manufacturing cost, advertising cost, and the size of market. Large markets can support relatively inexpensive books, while small markets require books that can carry higher prices. The most lucrative, and therefore the most attractive, books to publishers are those written for the undergraduate market. These books are usually "large" (expensive) and can be ordered in bulk lots.

THE CONTRACT

In journal publishing contractual terms are usually stated in a simple, straightforward letter of agreement. Other than remuneration, if any, the only significant question likely to arise is whether or not you, as author, hold the copyright to your article. In practice, many journals insist on holding all copyrights, not because of an anticipated financial gain, but because it simplifies their bookkeeping to have all of their material on the same legal footing. Journal publishers are generally quite willing to accommodate requests from authors to use or adapt their own articles and rarely charge for this. Publishers may charge someone other than the author, who wishes to borrow from the work. They also reserve the right to grant or withhold the request, and to pocket any fees levied.

Book contracts are more involved. Contracts for professional books are quite uniform and are much simpler than those for non-professional works such as novels. Contracts can vary on some important points, however, and these are worth description.

Copyright

Since 1978 a simplified copyright statute has been in effect that essentially vests the ownership of any creative work in the person or persons who created it, regardless of any subsequent publishing arrangements. The new law is actually simplified to the point that it has left considerable "gray areas" that will keep lawyers profitably employed for years to come, but these chiefly affect works that are more "artistic" than nursing books — plays, fiction, filmscripts — and will normally not complicate the lives of nursing authors and publishers. Since publishing contracts are written by publishers, they naturally reflect the publisher's point of view. Remember, contracts are basically agreements whereby authors hire professional companies to prepare their manuscripts for publication, manufacture, warehousing, promotion and distribution. It is true that most of the sales income comes back to the publisher, but so do most of the bills and virtually all of the risks of venturing capital in the first place. On average, a publisher ultimately **clears** slightly less income than the author.

There is one major exception to this publisher-as-service-agent arrangement. This is when a publisher **hires** an author or authors to complete a particular assignment such as the compilation of a reference book or revisions of a standard work whose original authors are deceased or otherwise *hors de combat*. This then is a "work for hire," and under such a set-up all rights are retained by the publisher.

Returning to the more common situation, the copyright may be registered either in the name of the author or the publisher. Under either arrangement the author's rights to a fair share of the profits remain intact, but there are two corollaries to the publisher's holding the copyright. The first, rather unlikely, is that the author might have to sue to get the money constituting a fair share. The legal expense, at least with most nursing books, would almost certainly be greater than the settlement awarded by a court. The obvious approach to this problem is prevention. Deal only with established publishers who are known to be ethical. A good reputation is of paramount importance in the publishing business.

The second corollary to a publisher-held copyright is that the negotiation of "derivative rights" rests entirely with the publisher. These are responsibilities that authors will want the experienced publisher to assume anyway and are generally ceded to it in other clauses of the contract, no matter in whose name the copyright is registered. Derivative rights cover special sales to bookclubs, foreign language editions, adaptations into other media like films, serialization or re-use of all or part of the book in journals or anthologies, etc. The publisher is obviously better prepared to negotiate the sale of such rights than an individual author. As an author, however, you should compare the various rates of sharing of income offered by different companies. You should also note whether such negotiations are subject to the author's approval, and request that prerogative if you feel strongly about it. (Even if it brings in some nice income, you may not want one of your chapters included in a book of readings compiled by someone you happen to loath.)

Since authors' approvals of such negotiations are sometimes needed (as a courtesy, if not legally) by the publisher on short notice, the number of authors signing a contract can represent a practical problem. Two or three, maybe four, authors are manageable; twenty-seven are not. Whether it is a matter of approving a bookclub sale or, at an earlier stage, deciding that a certain topic will or will not be treated in the book, the decision-making authority should be vested in as few people as possible. No nurse needs to be told what happens when decisions are left to committees.

What then happens when a large number of people are contributing to one book? The best arrangement from a logistic point of view is to keep the number of actual co-authors small and make the rest contributors. The simplest solution is to sub-contract with each of these contributing authors for a "work for hire" of the kind mentioned above, an assigned piece of writing which is purchased by the author(s) for a mutually agreed upon price, and all of the rights to which are then ceded to the author(s). The publisher can guide you in tailoring the details of such arrangements to your particular needs.

There are two other fundamental rights that figure prominently in publishing agreements: your right to enter into a contract to begin with, and the publisher's right to step aside if something you have written results in a lawsuit. The first of these has to do basically with plagiarism in its many interesting forms. Stated most simply, you must be perfectly sure before entering into a contract that the work you are proposing for publication is original and that your title to it is free and clear. Even if you have not yet put pen to paper, your **right** to do so may be questioned if your employer or former employer, be it a hospital, educational institution, governmental agency, private practice or professional organization, can claim that the knowledge, procedures or pedagogic techniques were generated at its behest while you were on its payroll. (Remember "works for hire?" This is what it looks like from the other side.) The diligent efforts of many workers notwithstanding, it is difficult not to learn *any*thing in the course of your job and to weave new knowledge into the broader fabric of your being. Thus the question of what is your own work and what is your employer's is subjective, and potentially acrimonious. In the interests of harmonious labor relations, and of avoiding lawsuits, it is best to air this question openly at the outset and set down clearly in writing the positions of all concerned if there has been any difference of opinion.

Then, if there **is** a difference of opinion resulting in litigation, you have the other basic right to be sued and to pay the legal costs whether or not you win. Every publishing contract contains a disclaimer which generously gives you this "right," and puts some distance between the publisher and any third party's attorneys. There are two primary reasons for a possible suit against an author. Plagiarism, as already noted, is one and harm resulting from directions or advice for improper or unsafe interventions with patients is the other. Publishers generally let authors deal with litigation on their own for two reasons. First, no matter how extensive their experience in the health-related sciences, publishers are limited in their ability to ascertain the originality of every bit of manuscript they process or its adequacy by professional nursing standards. Although in practice there will be one or more reviews of a manuscript, and especially any parts of it that seem questionable, publishers cannot be expected to know, for example, if a recommended procedure for turning a neurological patient might actually result in paralysis. Second, most instances of litigation arising out of a nursing publication are of the minor sort and can be most easily and cheaply settled out of court. However, the considerable assets of a legally vulnerable publisher provide an incentive for those who favor profit over justice to make as great an issue as possible out of the case, in the hope of getting a much larger settlement, in court or out. Few individual nurses have assets sufficient to make them worth suing for profit. Most publishers do, however, and they are understandably reluctant to become involved in legal gameplaying. If the author is obviously the innocent victim of a cynic or a crank, the odds are that the publisher will help out legally — but always short of the point of making itself a party to the grievance. This is small comfort to the would-be author, but sound survival instinct on the part of the publisher. Fortunately, commonsense helps prevent most conceivable lawsuits, and publishers **are** as helpful as they can be in avoiding them in the first place.

INCOME

Given the probability that you and your publisher agree that your book should be a money-making enterprise, the clauses of the contract governing income warrant close examination. To start with there is always a **basic edition**, usually the English-language edition first published in the United States, and it is with reference to this base unit that income is calculated or compared.

Royalties, although occasionally stated as a fixed fee per book sold, are almost always paid as a percentage of either the list price or the "net price" of the basic edition. The difference is substantial. The list price is the retail price recommended by the publisher, and on which its discounted prices to stores and wholesalers are figured. The net price, or "publisher's charges," is whatever the publisher is actually paid by customers in different discount brackets. These discounts range from none at all for the individual buying one copy of the book directly from the publisher, to a flat twenty percent for college bookstores, to more than fifty percent for those wholesalers who maintain certain inventory and cash volume levels, and who handle a very large part of all the nursing books sold. If your royalties are based on list price you always know where you stand. Even if the list price changes at some point, your percentage of the take remains constant. If your royalties are based on net price, demand to know in advance what the publisher's **average discount** is for your type of book. Without this knowledge you will have no way of knowing what your real share will be. For instance, if one publisher has offered you a base royalty of ten percent of list price and another has offered fifteen percent of net, but has an average discount of forty percent, the lower percentage in the first royalty actually represents more money. On a hypothetical $10.00 book ten percent of list is consistently $1.00, but fifteen percent of $10.00 minus forty percent is really fifteen percent of $6.00, or ninety cents.

Royalties also differ in being either flat or escalated. A flat royalty stays at the same percentage no matter how many copies of a book are sold, while the escalated royalty is raised at plateaus stated in the contract. The latter situation indirectly reflects the publisher's cash flow situation. Having invested initially a large sum of money in the book the publisher is primarily concerned with recouping this working capital for reinvestment in new book projects. Once this critical break-even point has been reached the publisher can breathe a little easier. Each subsequent copy sold not only begins clearing a profit, but a slightly increasing profit. After earning back a respectable amount for themselves some publishers will split the increased income with the author. As an example, the royalty might be ten percent of list price on the first fifteen thousand copies sold, eleven and a half percent on the next fifteen thousand, twelve and a half percent on the next ten thousand, and fourteen percent thereafter on all sales of a given edition. Since a revised edition costs

the publisher as much to produce as the first, the series of escala-
tions will revert to base level for each new edition. Too steep an
escalation, incidentally, is suspicious. If you have been offered terms
of fourteen or fifteen percent of net price on the first five thousand
copies and thirty percent thereafter, it is almost certain that the
publisher does not really anticipate sales above five thousand. The
book will, accordingly, be priced much higher than you expect. The
publisher expects to get what can be gotten from the book and then
kiss it goodbye; it could not expect to make a profit with a thirty
percent royalty on an average nursing book at an average discount
from an average list price.

Although it is not a very common situation in nursing (at
least by design) there are instances of zero royalties or even negative
royalties. In this case an author elects to take no income, or arranges
a subsidy from an outside source, in order to make possible the
publication of a work that would not be commercially viable otherwise. A worsening economic climate has affected governmental and
professional agencies, private philanthropies and even the profit
and loss statements of drug companies. Subsidies have in most cases
become fond memories. Thus many a noble, well-intentioned contribution to literature and civilization has to demonstrate its ability
to pay its own way.

In addition to income from the base royalty, there are also
special income categories listed in standard contracts. Even though
these royalties do not typically account for as much money as the
basic edition royalties they can, depending on the kind of book
involved, be significant. When shopping among publishers compare
the terms offered on special sales, both for the potential difference
in income they represent and also because they can reveal important
facts about the publishers themselves.

Foreign sales are the most obvious example. For most
American publishers the full base royalty is given on U.S. sales only.
A lower, unescalated royalty is given on sales in Canada and a
separate category identified for all other foreign sales, in English or
any other language. Publishers who must work through third parties to reach markets outside of the United States may in fact be
paying what amounts to a commission and thus have reason to
adjust royalties accordingly. You may well have reason to question
their selling power in these countries. Other publishers have affili-
ates in Canada and may service markets there adequately, in which
case your Canadian royalties should be comparable to the U.S.
terms. There is also a limited number of firms (including the pub-

lisher of this book) which consider "basic" the English-language edition of the book sold worldwide, and give the full royalty rate on all such sales.

Translation rights are usually sold to the highest bidder for each language or country, either on a royalty basis or for a lump sum. This is usually unaffected by the relationship — wholly-owned subsidiary to none at all — between the buying and selling publishers. The author's share may range from five or ten percent to fifty percent, so be alert and compare.

Bookclub sales do not normally generate much income, but do get a given title into the hands of nurses who do not live near specialized nursing or medical bookstores. Most often a club will buy a book from the publisher at the base manufacturing cost plus a royalty, usually a flat ten percent, keyed to their discounted list price. The major advantage to the publisher, if the sale is consummated prior to publication, is the increase thus permitted in the first printing and the consequent reduction in the cost per individual book as the total number goes up. The author may receive anything from five to fifty percent of the royalties, a big enough difference to warrant your haggling. You might want to inquire into a publisher's philosophy towards bookclubs, too. A very large publisher with a very large and expensive field sales force may legitimately feel that a bookclub sale of a textbook at a small profit detracts from its regular sales at relatively greater profit. At the other extreme, a publisher with little selling strength in nursing books may not even be able to consider a project unless part of the manufacturing expense is borne by a club. Every book is unique. Get the publisher's views on how your book will best be served before signing a contract. It is entirely possible that adoption of your book by a club as a major selection could mean more money in your pocket than the more modest sale, even at a higher royalty, that could be achieved through a sales force. In weighing these alternatives, bear in mind that more than half of all books sold in the U.S. today are sold through the mail.

The publisher's sales of other derivative rights of the kinds discussed previously — adaptation of the book into other media, inclusion in anthologies, etc. — will yield income shared with the author as much as fifty-fifty or as little as a congratulatory letter. Again, compare the terms offered.

Also check on the number of free copies you will receive on publication. These "freebies" are intended for your personal use — one to have bronzed, one to send to dear Aunt Nellie who always knew you would be either a great ventriloquist or a great author, etc., etc. You shouldn't be expected to supply complimentary promotional copies out of your own stock. This is the publisher's responsibility. On the other hand, you should not list the names of all of your personal friends as good sales prospects unless they really are likely to enhance the book's performance in the marketplace. Complimentary copies of books are a very expensive form of advertising and, since you do not earn any royalties on free copies, it is no less to your disadvantage than to the publisher's to give away the market. Therefore, you should not actually need a great many free copies for your own use unless you have an unusually large number of doting aunts or a great many contributing authors. In the latter case your contract should provide either that the contributors receive one or more free copies apiece, or are allowed to purchase personal copies at a preferential price.

There are two other forms of income that commonly appear in contracts and that are much more negotiable than other terms: **advances** and **grants.** An advance against future royalties is a loan, unsecured and non-interest-bearing, but repayable like any other loan — whether or not enough royalties are ever earned to cover it. Accordingly, both author and publisher ought to use common sense in such arrangements. It is generally accepted today that authors should not have to put up sizable sums of their own money to pay for the often considerable costs of professional typing, preparation of artwork, or telephone calls to contributors in far-flung places. However, it is still also wise not to borrow more than you or the publisher expect to earn back in a reasonable amount of time. If your editor blanches at the mention of a reasonable amount you should be wary of their sales expectations. However, if you mention an unreasonable amount you may wind up not negotiating at all, as editors tend to equate reasonable advance requests with reasonable authors and, therefore, nip unreasonable relationships in the bud.

A grant is an outright gift of cash made as an enticement to a highly desirable author to undertake a particularly attractive book. The money comes either straight out of the publisher's profit or, more frequently, out of the advertising budget. There are usually some strings attached to grants. The money may be doled out in segments as specified portions of the manuscript are submitted in finished form. If any of the money is designated for art preparation, the resulting illustrations, and occasionally the entire book, may become the property of the publisher. (In any subsequent misunderstanding it can be plausibly argued that it is a "work for hire.")

Finally, a grant is repayable if the author defaults on the contract
— something to bear in mind if you are mortal, subject to in-
capacitating illness or any other all too possible life crises. In practice, grants have become bargaining chips in the publishers'
competition for new titles. It is in the best interests of all parties to
temper short-term greed with long-term realism. If publishers give
away too much, the books suffer in the end. If authors overplay
their hands and demand too much, they will find that better publishers drop out of the bidding. Knowing when to stop bidding is
part of sound business judgment. There have been many instances
in which authors began by demanding more than they were worth
and ended up begging for whatever they could get.

One last word about royalties, advances and grants: they are
taxable as income during the year received, no matter when the
book comes out or is declared out of print. The structuring and
timing of your income, particularly from a "big" book, is something
you may want to discuss with your publisher before contracting.
Note too that you cannot, under present tax laws, deduct sums
spent on manuscript preparation (typing, photocopying, research-
related travel) as business expenses, as they are viewed as investments in what is expected to be a profitable enterprise.

When there is more than one individual involved in writing
a book the further complication of division of income arises. Deciding who has provided how much of the finished product is a ticklish
matter both before and after the work is done. Agatha Christie
observed long ago that she did not like to write with a collaborator
"because when two people are writing the same book each believes
he gets all the worries and only half of the royalties." Human nature
is quite predictable in such situations. Multiple authorship is, however, necessary to modern publishing and must be accounted for in
contracts. The simplest arrangement is that in which two or more
co-authors share equally the income and expenses resulting from
the book. Dividing things up unequally is also done routinely. As
long as the authors agree among themselves, the publisher will
accommodate their preferences. Contributors, as noted above, are
best paid off on a lump sum basis, although it is possible to assign
small percentages of the royalties to them. It is however undesirable
from the publisher's point of view to divide royalties among dozens
of authors and contributors as the bookkeeping expenses of keeping
track of numerous small accounts are disproportionately burden-
some.

Other Contract Terms

The remaining provisions of standard book contracts address themselves either to the obvious or to the unlikely, but a few points of practical significance should be examined and settled before you sign on the dotted line. Generally, the author's obligations to the publisher are much more carefully spelled out than the reverse and it is prudent to clarify ambiguous issues in a written amendment to the contract if necessary.

One of the most significant terms of the contract is the author's agreement to deliver a **complete** manuscript, including all artwork and permissions to use borrowed material, by a certain date **in content and form satisfactory to the publisher**. There are obvious hazards awaiting the unwary in these sweeping statements. A fundamental difference in roles needs to be emphasized: authors contract to write and publishers contract to publish. Today, while publishers still aim to restrict their activities to publishing proper, they are generally resigned to having to become involved to some extent in the authoring business as well, albeit reluctantly. Still, the following questions should be clear in your mind:

Who is responsible for completing the manuscript in "form satisfactory to the publisher." You are. If there are contributing authors, you are also responsible for their contributions. Besides the finished text, you are obligated to provide artwork prepared to the publisher's specifications, which normally means original black-on-white ink drawings and glossy photographs. If you wish to borrow existing material, either illustrations or text, from other works you are responsible for getting both reproduceable originals plus permission to use them. Any exceptions to the basic arrangement should be agreed to in writing.

Who is responsible for making sure the content is satisfactory to the publisher? Legally, the author is. This presupposes that your contract was based originally on a pre-existing table of contents and an estimated page length, and that you have not changed the scope, emphasis or dimensions of the book. However, it is a rare manuscript that does not undergo some natural growth, or shrinkage, and development during the gestation period. The important thing is to have your agreement on such changes confirmed in writing, and to keep all of the signed letters documenting these changes. Supporting correspondence becomes, in effect, additions to or revisions of the contract. The phrase "content and form satisfactory to the publisher" is necessary from the publisher's point of view to prevent nasty surprises, such as a 20-page pamphlet when a 750-page textbook was expected, or a book on some other topic entirely. Unfortunately this phrase has also been used and abused as an "escape clause."

Who is responsible for editing the manuscript?   The contract obligates you to provide the publisher with a comprehensible and grammatical text written in something readily identifiable as your common native language. As this ideal is sometimes not attained, most publishers retain the right (but usually **not** the legal obligation) to edit the manuscript to conform to certain standards. Such standards can cover a lot of ground. Some publishers feed "raw" copy to the typesetter and are blithely indifferent to the quality — or lack of quality — of the prose that results. Some go to the other extreme, performing major surgery on a manuscript, usually felt by the author to be an operation without benefit of anesthesia. Extremes of this sort may or may not be justified in specific cases and may or may not please both participants. There are two keys to harmony. First, prior to contracting, write a sample chapter and ask that it be edited, so both parties know what to expect. Second, be sure to **maintain a dialogue** with your editor so that expectations do not diverge.

Who is responsible for indexing the book?   Since indexing is the last job to be done on a manuscript before manufacturing it is often not thought of before it arises. It is almost always the author's privilege to handle this chore. Few publishers do indexing "in-house," but they will gladly sub-contract with a professional indexer for you — at your expense. The cost, usually treated as an advance against royalties, can be considerable, running into thousands of dollars for a big textbook. Doing your own index is not really all that difficult, especially if the publisher is reasonably cooperative, but it is always by definition a "rush job" since all other work on the book must cease until it is finished. It is also a very boring job. The best solution will differ according to circumstances, but the pros and cons in your case can at least be examined beforehand and your editor should always warn you of the approximate expense in advance.

Who is responsible for advertising and promotion?   This, at least, is the publisher's obligation. It is also often a bone of contention. Mutual expectations ought to be voiced soon enough for you to foresee and resolve any disagreements. The contract usually dwells rather lightly on the publisher's responsibility, saying only something to the general effect that it promises to market and promote the work as it sees fit. Authors usually have a different perspective as they are unaware of the ever-increasing costs of advertising. It is almost impossible for the publisher to give an author a finished promotion plan much before publication, but there is always a budget and tentative plan for how the advertising money can best be spent. The editor can describe the plan in general terms, and will probably solicit your help in refining it. A close working relationship based on realistic expectations should result in mutual satisfaction.

Who is responsible for getting the book out on schedule?   All book contracts have the author's "manuscript due date" spelled out very clearly and give the publisher a distinct advantage in stipulating that the manuscript be **complete** by then. This is fair as far as it goes because the publisher, juggling the schedules of dozens or hundreds of books simultaneously, cannot really meet deadlines if significant parts of the manuscript are not submitted on time. However, authors are not the only culprits when it comes to tardiness. There are two points on which prior understandings are essential. One is that the publisher also should have a deadline, usually twelve months from receipt of the finished manuscript. Some contracts casually omit this bit of protection for the author. The other point, if it comes up at all, is that the publisher should not be able to postpone its deadline unreasonably on the basis of a technicality. For example, if you submit a manuscript complete except for an unfinished illustration or a delayed permission to use copyright material, a decent publisher will make allowances. A publisher really cannot, however, accept a manuscript with a thousand "loose ends" dangling. If you have kept the publisher informed of progress and problems, you can usually rely on receiving understanding and help.

Who decides the physical format and price of the book?   The publisher reserves this right, but the author obviously has a say in it. The question of format is integral to the overall conceptualization of the book and therefore an appropriate and necessary topic of discussion during your earliest negotiations. The publisher, knowledgeable of manufacturing and promotional costs and the nature of the market, can determine the optimal "packaging" and pricing of the book easily. Authors who have not yet familiarized themselves with the economics generally find prices too high. One almost universal misunderstanding is that paperbacks are very much cheaper to manufacture than clothbound books. Not so. It is relatively inexpensive to do a paperback edition **after** the hardbook has been published and the initial investment earned back. With an original edition of a book the difference in manufacturing cost between cloth and paper covers is modest. The public expects generally that paperbacks will be cheaper than hardbooks. Since it will not much affect the price anyway, it is sometimes better to give them a durable clothbound "bargain" than what seems an unreasonably expensive paperback.

Who is responsible for new editions?   Contract terms on this vary, but generally the publisher must decide that a revision is warranted and the author is obligated to arrange to do it within a specified time after being asked. Conversely, if the author feels a new edition is needed the publisher should be subject to a similar obligation. If the author is unable or unwilling to come up with a satisfactory schedule, or any schedule, for a revision of a successful book, the publisher often reserves the right to protect its investment by hiring someone else to do the job. You should check the contract terms carefully to see that in such a case you (or your estate, as this situation is actually most likely to arise after you have achieved literary immortality) are still recompensed fairly for that part of the revision which is your original contribution.

If the publisher is unable or unwilling to undertake a new edition, you should be sure that it is contractually obligated to turn its rights back over to you so that you are free to try to place the book with another publisher. The odds are that if one publisher does not think it profitable to revise the book, neither will others. There is, however, no reason why the publisher should deprive you of the opportunity. Similarly, the contract should provide for reversion of all rights to the author in the event (uncommon, but not unheard of) that the publisher goes out of business.

What claim does the publisher have to any future work of yours?   Some contracts give the publisher what is called "the right of first refusal," the exclusive right to publish your next book if it chooses. As a matter of principle, you ought to refuse to accept this clause. If you and the publisher have served each other well there will be no need for it. If things have not gone smoothly, then a forced reenactment is not a good solution.

WHAT TO EXPECT

The somewhat cynical tone of this chapter has been deliberate. At its best publishing will be a gratifying and rewarding experience, but this presupposes that the author has at least a general knowledge of the process, and an appreciation of both parties' obligations. Authors in nursing usually do not. In general nurses are more motivated by good intentions than other groups. They assume that they will be dealt with honorably.

Publishing, for its part, is much more honorable in its dealings than, say, an oil cartel. It is populated by well educated people who are quite aware that they could be earning more money in some less genteel business. It is also a business that has been particularly hard hit by the adverse economic trends of recent years. Under these circumstances gentility has had to come to terms with pragmatism. When the ultimate owners of a publishing company can get a higher yield on their investment by putting it into savings bonds, the company's employees learn quickly to distinguish between that which would be nice to publish and that which will be profitable. There is less flexibility, the bargaining becomes harder, and the importance of mutual understanding between authors and publishers becomes greater. If the restraints and ground rules are not mutually accepted and respected the author/editor relationship can become an adversarial one. Under these circumstances it is especially important to appreciate the real problems you will encounter:

There is never enough time to write.   Actually anyone who is doing something well enough to justify writing about it lacks the time to do so by definition. The time must be **created**. Furthermore, it must be created in spite of the callous indifference of your family, employer, colleagues and virtually all significant others in your life who view your taking time away from **them** as selfishness. Such is the price of literary fame. Set aside **blocks** of time on a regular basis and guard them jealously, otherwise you will begin to fall behind schedule and the joy of writing will become drudgery. This is a "no-win" situation to be avoided at all costs.

You never know as much about your topic as you think.   Writing, like all forms of teaching, has a discomfiting way of revealing gaps in your knowledge. This is only normal, but unfortunately you cannot just let it go at that. The gaps must be filled. For this you must marshall adequate resources. Access to a good library is essential. You should have available such basic references as a standard English dictionary, a nursing and/or medical encyclopedia, any basic texts in your field to which you will refer repeatedly, and a guide to English composition. Access to human resources is important too. Be careful however that in seeking the advice of consultants or in relying on the writings of others you don't abuse the privilege. To Lionel Trilling's observation that "Immature artists imitate, mature artists steal" might be added the caveat that responsible authors give credit where it is due — and do not undertake a book at all if they don't know enough about the subject.

No one else attaches the same importance to your manuscript that you do. Typists are notoriously blasé about losing pages of your handwritten draft. They may also take considerable liberties with the vocabulary you have used. Artists, especially amateurs, look upon a book as a vehicle to demonstrate their unrecognized gifts and are not about to let your text interfere with what *they* think ought to be emphasized in the illustrations. The Post Office, though blamed unfairly for all sorts of things, has consigned more than one manuscript to oblivion. They routinely vent repressed aggressive tendencies on any parcel marked "Photographs — Do Not Bend." Never send the only draft of a manuscript through the mail. Pack everything defensively and send it registered. Get professional references for typists, artists and especially contributors.

No one else likes your writing style as much as you do.   Although most authors, experienced or not, seek the support of good copyediting, seeing your own manuscript dripping with red pencil marks is at best accompanied by a twinge of pain and at most by an egotistical tantrum. This can be due to poor or arbitrary copyediting — who will ever understand why some manuscript editors change every "that" to a "which" and others do just the reverse? However, extensive rewording and even reorganizing of a manuscript more often is due to the simple fact that the original writing is execrable. The poet, e.e. cummings was prematurely optimistic when, on the death of President Harding, he observed that we had lost the only man, woman or child who wrote a simple declarative sentence with seven grammatical errors.*[17]

Much of the problem derives from an all but universal feel-

*From an undocumented source in Stephan Pile's *The Incomplete Book of Failures* (NY: E.P. Dutton, 1979). Harding's posthumous (and ungrammatical) retort — "What the hell would some smart alec poet who can't tell that little letters are different from big ones know anyways?" is even more undocumented.

ing among nurses that writing should either be extremely ornate, ponderous and ultrapedantic or, more rarely, slangy, colloquial and "telling it like it is." Moderation is the best course. Nursing as a profession depends on clear, specific and efficient communication. In writing, as in speaking, you should strive for directness, economy and that degree of formality that distinguishes a professional consultation from a coffee klatch. Avoid affectations, cute language and trendy "buzz" words likely to be out of vogue before the book is published. Stick to simple, declarative sentences (preferably without seven grammatical errors). If you believe something and can document the basis of your belief, say it. Similarly, avoid betraying a lack of confidence in yourself by repeating the same point four different ways.

As a rule, publishers are happy when little editing is needed. Manuscript editing is time-consuming and expensive. The copyeditor's responsibility includes routine correction of grammar, spelling, style and rephrasing for clarity. It does not include license to change your meaning (unless this has been demonstrated to be wrong). Where one of your statements seems too general or vague, incompatible with other parts of the manuscript, or of questionable accuracy, the copyeditor can and should challenge it, and you should answer that challenge fully. Where the copyeditor has gratuitously altered your meaning and you know you are right, restore your original statement. The copyeditor's role is that of devil's advocate, of trying to anticipate the reader's reaction to the text. You as author are the authority. This distinction should never be blurred. Remember too that your editor is still **your** advocate and is obliged to stand by you during the entire editing process.

It is easier to raze than to praise.   Upon its release copies of your book are (or should be) sent by the publisher to all journals with a potential interest in it. This bit of ritual masochism is more often than not a "no-win" situation. Bad reviews hurt — you, if not sales. Good reviews typically appear months after publication, in the wrong journals, and rarely precipitate a stampede on local bookstores. There are several defenses and offenses for this problem. "Those who can, write; those who can't, review," uttered at strategic moments in the right company may not do much to improve sales but it provides some comfort to your bruised ego. More constructively, identify individuals who regularly review for appropriate journals and see that the publisher sends a freebie to each such reviewer. Also, cultivate contacts in high places either directly or through your publisher. These contacts could be officers of your specialized professional organization, other successful authors or people who just get around and talk a lot. If these people themselves are potential reviewers, a flattering little personal note sent with the review copy cannot hurt. If, more likely, they can **recommend** good reviewers, such leads should be followed through. Send notes that say "President so-and-so of our Association has suggested that you would be interested in reviewing my new book because of our similar backgrounds and interests." The important thing is to try if possible to get an ally interested in doing the review and so advising the journal before someone else does. Someone else may turn out to be a competing author with an ax to grind. Since the "system" is arbitrary and unfair, you may as well tip the scales in your favor whenever you can.

The book never sells as many copies as you expect, especially at first. This is a fact of life. You are more interested in your topic than others or you wouldn't be writing about it. The temptation to believe that "everybody will buy this book" is always there, but you would be well advised to hold off spending your first royalty check until after it arrives. On a more positive note, nursing books generally tend to do better in their second year than in the first, reflecting a general conservatism in the profession. Also, advances, contributors' payments, indexing charges and the like are deducted from your first royalties, so things usually get more profitable as they go along. Of course, if they get **too** profitable you will quite likely find that imitation is the most lucrative form of flattery and that three clones of your book follow its publication by about two years. Take heart; just as your imitators have tried to improve on your work, you can learn from their successes and failures and outdo **them** with your second edition. The intelligent planner with reasonable expectations can still do reasonably well financially.

Is it all worth it? It is if approached with worth, in its broadest sense, in mind. Bearing unforeseen technological breakthroughs that would considerably reduce manufacturing costs, books will continue to go up in price. This will not render them obsolete, despite the prophecy years ago by Marshall McLuhan that books were a dying breed. (Professor McLuhan has since died; books are still published.) Books **will** be greater financial risks, however. Authors who understand the economics of publishing are more likely to achieve results that satisfy both themselves and the publisher.

You have already taken one wise economic step in buying this book. Among other things you have saved yourself the considerable cost of a literary agent if you do decide to write. You have been warned of both the pitfalls, and the paths around them — keys to **designing** a profitable publication from the beginning. The author of the present book, with a keen appreciation of the value of time and money, has written before and did not hesitate to do so again. With the reassurance of sound guidance and reassuring examples of success, there is nothing holding **you** back.

IV INVESTING IN OTHERS — INTRODUCTION

THERE ARE THREE main objectives for investment; to protect your capital or principal, to provide income or a
rate of return, and to provide appreciation or increase the value of
your investment capital. There is, however, no ideal investment,
one that meets all three objectives. Investment priorities can and
usually do change. Safety of capital and income may be the priority
objectives as you become older. Therefore, it is important to evaluate your investment objectives continuously and make the appropriate adjustments.

There is no perfect low risk, high return investment. Nothing and no one can guarantee successful investment; it is always
speculative. The ability to invest is directly related to earnings,
discretionary income and willingness to take a risk. If all your salary
or income is needed to meet day-to-day expenses your investment
ability, unless you choose to go into debt, is limited. The only
investment choices may be those described in earlier chapters; education, image and appearance, or career change.

Chapters 10, 11 and 12 focus on several common forms of
investment; securities, real estate, and insurance. These chapters are
not intended to give definitive answers, or even to tell you all you
want or need to know. They do provide an overview, key points,

and helpful hints. There are, of course, many other types of investments; savings accounts, coins, stamps, works of art, antiques, commodities and trust funds. Whichever investment you choose, you will want to minimize the risk and maximize the return on investing. Before putting out your hard earned dollars in any investment that you do not control directly, you should seek expert advice, shop around, and know what you are doing! Any investment, like a vegetable garden, requires constant attention and work; either yours or someone else's. So be prepared to invest time as well as dollars. After all, if it were easy we would all be millionaires by now.

*No man but feels more of a man in
the world if he can have a bit of
ground that he can call his own.
However small it is on the surface, it
is four thousand miles deep; and that
is a very handsome property.*
CHARLES DUDLEY WARNER

10 Investing in Real Estate

J. R. Salisbury

MANY DISCERNING BUSINESS PEOPLE consider investment
in real estate the simplest and safest guard against inflation. The value of real estate usually rises with inflation and continues as its own future security. In other words, appreciation, or
increase in value of the capital investment, is the chief advantage
of real estate. Another advantage is the tax deduction allowed for
interest payments on mortgages. These tax advantages can be considerable, particularly in the beginning years of the mortgage.

A chief disadvantage to real estate is relatively poor liquidity. It may take many months or even years to turn your real estate
into cash. Soaring mortgage interest rates and tight money markets
may make selling even more difficult. Also, real estate investments
in urban areas are thought to be high risks today because of the
deteriorating quality of life, escalating insurance costs and reduction
in fire and policy protection for property. However, with careful
searching and consideration of personal objectives, there is something available in the real estate market to suit virtually every taste
and need related to size, location, privacy, maintenance, upkeep
requirements, financing and, all important — price.

Real estate should continue to be a good investment as there
is increasing demand for living accommodations in a restricted

157

number of geographical areas. Also, inflationary costs of building new properties increase the value of existing houses and apartments. A final factor, the continuing preference of young and old people to live outside the nuclear family, maintains the demand for additional living units. Gone are the days when grandparents, parents, and children all lived in the same home for all or most of their lifetimes.

PRIVATE HOME OWNERSHIP

Owning a home is often considered the ultimate American dream. Before making the actual purchase, you should read the real estate ads covering the geographic area in which you're most interested. In this way you'll familiarize yourself with the general price ranges as well as with the names of local realtors with whom you may want to do business. Generally, real estate advertisements appear toward the end of the week and on weekends, when the greatest activity in house hunting seems to take place. It's always informative and usually a pleasant outing to visit advertised "open houses." This helps you become familiar with both the real estate market in general, and the varying costs in the specific area. Use a realtor who is a member of the National Association of Realtors (NAR) to assist you in your search. They know what is available locally and the housing market in general. Properties may be exclusive listings or multiple listings. Your realtor will know. Real estate is like any other investment — it is wise to use the services of experts in your decision making.

Price is of course important, but it is not the only variable in the final decision. First, determine the location and size house desired. That super house you find in the suburbs at a bargain price could prove to be an expensive white elephant if it's too large, and too far away from your job and the activities you enjoy. Accessability to shopping, schools, church, entertainment, and public transportation is important too. Although your car is faithfully getting you back and forth now, who knows when the next gas crunch may come. There is also that unanticipated inconvenient occasion when old faithful just won't start.

Frequently a large, older and slightly fading dowager of a home is a fantastic buy. The original workmanship in a quality older home is usually far superior to today's construction. The use of handsome paneling and lavish moldings in these structures also has great appeal for many people interested in the splendor of yester-day's buildings. These amenities are seldom found today, because they are too costly in both labor and materials. "Doing-it-yourself" can be a fine economic as well as ego rewarding project. This is particularly true if the house is situated in a neighborhood that has always enjoyed a "choice" or a better-than-average reputation, shows every promise of continuing in that category, and has evidence of concern and pride on the part of surrounding property owners. Don't expect, however, to reap 100% in resale on modernization costs, even though they undoubtedly enhance the property and advertise to its value. Realistically you will recover approximately 50% of alteration costs. For example, a $2600 kitchen remodeling will add roughly $1300 to the future selling price. Determine the amount you will have to budget for repairs, renovations and redecoration **after** purchase price, closing costs, insurance and taxes. Also, it is wise to get a list of local repair men and odd-job persons who are familiar with work that has been needed in the past and who will be available when needed again.

If a new home most interests you, remember that the integrity and reliability of the builder is an important factor to consider. Check with people who are presently occupying dwellings constructed by this firm or individual. If the home you're inspecting is a model, don't be overly impressed by the eye catching additions or decorations. These may not be a part of each future home. Don't take for granted **any** statements about features of the house, the exact size of the lot, the completion date of construction, or the standards of quality of the furnished equipment such as appliances or plumbing fixtures. Any of these items or any requested and agreed-upon changes in the basic house should be spelled out in writing.

Find out the zoning regulations for your purchase area, even if it appears to be strictly residential. It may, in fact, be zoned for commercial usage, a zoning that could adversely affect property values now or in the future. Check with the local government offices, not with the builder's representative or a future neighbor.

A real estate investment that can also supplement your income each month is a multiple dwelling. You're almost guaranteed that the tenant's rent payment will carry your real estate taxes as well as almost all of the maintenance costs. You **do** forfeit some privacy in this arrangement, but you at least get to select who will be sharing your privacy.

Maintenance and upkeep may also be a problem. However,

it is possible to hire a "superintendent" of sorts, either on a daily basis or as a resident of your building. The financial arrangement is often a reduced rental rate for services rendered or specialized jobs around the property. Get this agreement in writing or have it specifically detailed in his written lease. This arrangement provides immediate help on hand for day to day emergencies while you're at work. You are also free to get away occasionally for a weekend or vacation with confidence that all will be taken care of on the home front. This arrangement provides a most important pleasure of home ownership, enjoyment of property, without the extra work which ownership entails. You know that your "super" will mow the lawn, shovel the snow and take care of small repair problems. Virtually every city and town has attractive homes that have been converted to multi-family use. Once again, be sure to check the immediate and surrounding neighborhood on several different occasions for general appearance, upkeep and evidence of pride in ownership.

You've finally found the right size house in the right location. Next, you should have the property checked out and appraised. Locate a qualified real estate appraiser. Look for the initials M.A.I. (Member of Appraisal Institute), R.M. (Residential Member), or S.R.A. (Senior Residential Appraiser) after the appraiser's name. These initials indicate the person is certified and meets certain standards. He'll evaluate the property for a fee and give an unbiased opinion of the market value. You can also expect an inspection of the plumbing, electrical wiring, heating system, insulation, termite infestation, and anything else you request as necessary.

Find out from the neighbors, the real estate broker, or city hall if any changes are anticipated in the neighborhood, such as sewers, roads or new schools. These changes can affect the ambiance of the neighborhood as well as your taxes and even your landscaping. For additional help in knowing what to look for you may want to write for the booklet entitled "Basic Housing Inspection." It can be obtained free from U.S. Department of Health and Human Services, Room 1587, Parklawn Building, 5600 Fishers Lane, Rockville, Maryland 20852.

Sylvia Porter's *New Money Book for the 80's* includes in Chapter 5 excellent detailed check lists for comparing potential home purchases. There is no reason to buy a pig in a poke, especially when it will be such an expensive "pig."

Investment in real property is an important and expensive decision. To maximize the investment success and minimize the risk you should use real estate experts and lawyers. To buy property directly from a seller without the aid of a licensed real estate broker or salesman may prove highly risky. Use a lawyer to determine the legality of your purchase, the correctness of the contract and to close the sale. You will, of course, have to pay fees for these services but it is worth the price to avoid problems in the future.

What Can You Afford and How Should You Finance?

To be realistic about what you can afford, ask a savings and loan institution or your present bank to estimate the potential mortgage available based on your income, current debts, credit history and job security. You can also make your own rough estimate by following the form in table 10-1. There is some evidence that the old rule of thumb, allowing for a maximum allocation of 25% of income for real estate debt, is being increased to 28%.

In the present economic climate, the mortgage market is unpredictable. The availability of mortgage money, the price or interest charges for this money, and the terms of payment change on a daily basis. As this chapter was being written mortgage interest rates fluctuated back and forth several times. Your ultimate goal is to invest the least amount of capital in property and to earn the greatest percentage return. This approach is often called "leverage." Achieving leverage may be more difficult today because of the demands for initially high down-payments. For example, a $100,000 home with a mortgage of $50,000 will yield a better return if the value increases in the first year by 10% ($10,000 increase on $50,000 equals 20% increase in equity) than if the mortgage was $30,000 ($10,000 on $70,000 investment yields 14 2/3%)

Getting a bargain is also a desirable goal. Prices of home real estate tend to be higher in the spring and fall months. Shopping in the off season can yield either a lower initial price or a better deal when present owners become anxious about selling.

Interest rates tremendously affect what your home will ultimately cost. Home mortgage rates have soared in the past few years and don't seem to be coming down. This means you may pay back over the period of the mortgage many, many times the actual amount borrowed. For example, if you borrow $20,000 at 16% for

10 years you will pay back approximately $70,000! A few percentage points make a considerable difference and therefore interest rate is critical.

Inquire about the availability of special mortgages, such as "take-over" — one in which you assume the present mortgage at the original interest rate. Banks, of course, will not be eager to tell you about these, but they do exist. You may also be eligible for a F.H.A. (Federal Housing Authority) or Veterans Administration loan, both of which have better terms for the buyer.

There are also special types of mortgages such as Graduated Payment, Reverse Annuity, Variable Rate, and Rollover or Renegotiable Mortgages. The details of each of these need to be investigated and compared. The availability will vary regionally. Lawyers, brokers and bankers can help you find out as much as possible before making your decision.

In addition to the interest and principal payments, you can expect some extras such as "points" or the amount deducted from the face value of your mortgage. For example if the lender charges you three points on a $20,000 mortgage you either get only $19,400 (but must pay back $20,000 plus interest) or you pay $600 "up front."

Closing costs, or the dollars charged for legal fees, insurance, taxes, mortgage processing fees etc. also must be paid in cash at the time of closing. Mortgage terms vary and need to be clarified. Can you pay off the mortgage early? If so, how much of a penalty must you pay? How late can your mortgage payment be without a penalty? What kind of mortgage insurance is required? Ask your legal advisor and the lending institution to clarify these points for you. Two things, however, are relatively certain. You will need a considerable cash down-payment and will pay an interest rate that is quite high (unless you are lucky enough to find a take-over mortgage). As with other investments you will need to shop around to find the financing that is available and affordable.

The Federal Home Loan Bank Board, which oversees federal savings and loan associations, has instituted several proposals aimed at benefiting first time buyers as well as lenders. More and more individual sellers are taking back second mortgages privately at attractive interest rates. Occasionally, too, realtors will have knowledge of agencies offering second mortgages. A second mortgage is, as its name indicates, representative of any difference between the required down payment and the sum the lending institution will allow as your mortgage.

Second Homes: Are They for You?

Are you in the market for a second home such as a vacation cottage or seasonal dwelling? Your personal financial picture will determine if you must settle on a property that is readily rentable during the weeks and months when you'll not be using the house. If you have an aversion to short-term tenants moving in and out on a bi-weekly or even weekly basis, and you're in the position of not needing the added income to help carry the house, you are fortunate!

Many owners who can well afford to keep their hideaway totally private, still prefer an off-season resident in their home. If it is secluded, or even if not, there is the constant worry of a possible break-in. Very often, it's sensible to find a full time tenant at a reduced monthly rental for the months you are absent. The loss of income is offset by the comfort of knowing your investment is being looked after. You may be able to rent ten months of the year to a local school teacher, or a young couple attending a nearby college. If your personal use of a seaside home will be three or four weeks each summer, you must decide if you'll want the prime time for yourself or would rather select the less desirable weeks and reap the benefits of a greater rental income. Many places have the bonus of two vacation periods, as for example a summer resort on a New England lake where skiing is also available nearby all winter long. In this situation, you not only have the added use of your home in other seasons (spring and fall are great vacation times in so many areas), but there is an additional and significant rental potential.

The last thing you'd want is to be a slave to maintenance in a second home. Be sure you don't involve yourself with too much yard to care for, too much house to paint, or antiquated plumbing that has a short and erratic future. Remember, this is to be your "get away from it all" spot, so don't tie yourself down to a place that will demand all of your spare time.

Another consideration is that when rented, the property may provide you with tax free income by your using allowable deductible expenses and depreciation. Since the regulations change on these allowances from year to year, seek guidance from your tax accountant or the Internal Revenue Service. For example, your cabin in the New Hampshire woods, paid in full cash, is used by you for one month, rented for two months and unoccupied the remaining nine. Your yearly expenditures include property taxes and the cost of necessary maintenance and upkeep. There is an annual depreciation allowance, calculated as if the house were declining in value each year, when in fact it will probably be increasing quite handsomely. For the three months that the house is 'in season' and capable of producing income, you apply the total yearly expenses of taxes, necessary maintenance and depreciation, pro-rated for two of those three months, or the time of actual rental. From your rental income, you may deduct two thirds of these expenses, thus paying tax on only a small percentage of your cash profit. Even if your deductions for expenses exceed your rental income, there are special tax rules that apply, still with tax benefits in many cases.

CONSIDERING CONDOMINIUMS AND CO-OPERATIVES

If the responsibility for a privately owned property is more than you want, you may wish to consider a co-op or condominium instead. The increasingly popular "condo" is a form of ownership of a garden apartment, high rise or connected town house, in which you buy physical space in a larger structure and have joint ownership with other resident owners of the halls, basement, stairs, and other common areas. In contrast, in a cooperative you buy shares of stock, representative of the size of the unit you elect, in a corporation that owns the entire building. Frequently banks will charge an additional 1 to 1½ points on mortgage loans for cooperatives because you are purchasing shares of stock rather than real estate itself. Obtaining a mortgage for a co-op or condominium may be more expensive and difficult than for a private dwelling, depending on where you are buying and what the money market is like. You will need to obtain a copy of the prospectus. Read it carefully and have your attorney review it for your obligations and privileges. The same kind of questions and factors that were indicated about private home buying apply to co-ops and condominiums. In addition you need to investigate the reputation and financial responsibility of the real estate management company.

There is a monthly maintenance fee in both co-ops and condos and possibly a monthly assessment in case of damage to any of the common rooms. There is usually an owners' association in both co-ops and condos to protect the rights of the individual owners. The condominium association will have an elected board of directors administering through a set of governing by-laws. The board hires a building manager, insurers, accountants, lawyers and office staff. If the development is not well run, maintained and financially supported, the entire project and your personal investment could be jeopardized.

If you are elected a director you personally should have liability insurance as protection against any negligence suits brought against the board. Being a director may take much more of your time and energy than you formerly devoted to the management of your own private home. However, the cost of condominiums on the average is less than houses, therefore giving you a potentially better value for your money. Condominiums do seem to appreciate at a slower rate than houses, however, except where the real estate market is booming. You can probably expect to move into your condo, live there comfortably for some time, and realize a nice profit on moving out, providing the building and its reputation have been kept in good repair!

Condominiums offer a happy combination of owning and sharing, and privacy and "togetherness." Condos usually attract a certain type of resident; couples of or near retirement age, younger childless couples, singles, and sports loving folks who spend every spare hour at the community pool, tennis courts or golf course. Some owners are uninterested in these extras and would rather see their maintenance fees used for other services. Remember, even if you don't take advantage of these facilities yourself, you help finance them. Often buyers are unaware that when they buy, the recreation facilities belong to the developer, not the condo owners. The developer may raise the monthly charges as he deems necessary. It is wise to think seriously about these recreational facilities, or lack of them, in any development you're considering. Remember that operating costs, to which you contribute through your monthly assessment fee, will often exceed projected figures, possibly even doubling in amount! The fees may have been set too low originally in order to attract buyers.

Determine if your builder intends to enlarge the development in the future. Such construction may change the appearance of the complex as a whole, or may put another building adjacent to yours, blocking that beautiful view which was the determining factor in selection of your unit! Make a complete list of questions for the developer as you examine your prospective condo. Are there any restrictions on pets? Can you rent your unit if you want to? Are most of the residents owners or are there an appreciable number of tenants (renters of units owned by others)? As a rule, owner-occupancy provides better control.

How are utility costs covered? Are appliance warranties given? What is the parking situation? Is there storage space provided? What is the trash disposal arrangement? Is carpeting required? (This could make an important difference to you, especially if the people upstairs practice the tango nightly.) For more detailed information on condominium regulations, write to the attorney general's office, the consumer protection agency in your state, or the Community Associations Institute, 1832 M. Street, N.W., Washington, D.C., for their pamphlet designed for condominium buyers.

A variation on the condo theme is the "vacation condo," a trend enjoying great popularity in vacation areas all over the United States, Europe, and Mexico. Some of these vacation condos have been planned as family-type communities and not resorts, simply because they have the good fortune to be located in a spot conducive to vacationing. A word of caution! Check the local vacancy rate carefully. In certain resort areas there has been substantial over-building necessitating drastic measures on the part of some builders to promote sales of their empty condominiums.

"Time Sharing" is a leisure home concept whereby you own a portion of a year's time in an apartment or single dwelling unit, and are guaranteed specific weeks every year, according to the amount of your investment. You may also be able to select other holiday facilities in resorts affiliated with your parent company by trading in your own appointed weeks. Each plan varies in the scheduling system used for exchange. These schedules may be complicated, requiring careful study. Considerable advance notice and many forms are also usually required. Fees are charged for annual dues and special services.

SHARING A REAL ESTATE INVESTMENT

Consult your attorney first!! The expansion of the popular idea of sharing an investment, whether purchase or rental, calls for a greatly increased legal awareness of problems associated with this phenomenon.

The initial financial advantages are well defined and very appealing. The initial investment, purchase price or monthly rental is shared with another person or persons. Future maintenance and household costs are also shared, making your own contribution one-half or less of what it might be if you were doing it on a solo basis. It is also a relief to know that the entire weight and responsibility do not rest on your shoulders.

Whether or not you want the mixed burden and pleasure of sharing will ultimately depend, of course, on your own desire and need for independence. Recent credit laws make it possible to buy a home with a non-related individual, using your combined incomes as a financial basis on which the mortgage loan will be extended. With the help of an accountant, determine your monthly housing expenses. Ask his advice on the tax deductible interest on your share. Your monthly costs may be reduced appreciably, depending on your tax bracket. A conventional mortgage loan today requires at least 20% to 30% of the purchase price as a down payment. In this unsettled time of constantly changing money markets and new types of mortgages, the advice of your accountant and real estate agent will prove invaluable. Always consult your lawyer. What seems to be the ideal merger now may turn out to be quite the opposite in the future. Legal advice at the outset will save you anguish if the friendly relationship with your "partner" deteriorates.

RENTALS

You may be one of the many millions of individuals who have no interest in or financial capability of owning a home of any sort. There are many types of appropriate rental opportunities, although in some cities they are becoming increasingly difficult to find. Approach your search for a rental in the same way already outlined for a purchase. Read the newspaper ads, look for signs on property advertising "For Rent," use a real estate office listing, or ask your friends and co-workers. Once you let it be known that you're searching for something to rent, you'll be surprised at the response. People will tell you, "I know of an apartment on the third floor of my building that will be available next month," or "Jane Adams, at the Apex Real Estate Office, is the person to see. They have several nice homes for rent, furnished or unfurnished, as well as apartments in converted homes from time to time. She found our place for us." Or, "My Aunt Maribell has a vacancy in her three family building on Front Street, and I know she'd be happy to have you as a tenant." In the "big city" you can let the doormen or superintendents of desirable buildings know you are looking (and don't forget to give them some financial reward for their help).

Table 10-1. A Rough Estimate of Your Possible Expenses

To figure approximately what you will be able to spend, itemize your expenses in a schedule like the following:

Monthly food and household costs _____

Insurance _____

Transportation _____

Clothing _____

Education _____

Health Costs _____

Installment and debt payments _____

Entertainment and vacation _____

Personal Expenses _____

Taxes (not withheld from pay) _____

Telephone _____

Charities _____

Savings _____

Any Other _____

Total: $ _____

To be subtracted from your monthly income of:

Take home pay (after taxes) _____

Other income _____

Total: $ _____

(1) Amount Available for Housing:

With some previous idea of the down payment you can afford, coupled with the amount you'll probably be able to spend following this guide, you can now consider the actual real estate offerings. When you've located something of interest, make another list showing the expected monthly expenses relative to that property:

Mortgage   _____
Property Taxes   _____
Insurance   _____
Repairs and Maintenance (about
  one twelfth of one percent of
  the selling price)   _____
Utilities and Heating   _____
Other   _____

(2) **Total Projected Expenses:** $ _____

Now compare the totals of (1) and (2). If (1) is larger than (2), you've found a prospective property within your budget!

You may seriously consider spending more if you anticipate any increase in your income, if you have other sources of emergency revenue, or if the selling price is appreciably below that of comparable properties. But if your down payment will be low, you think there might be an addition (or two!) to your family in the near future, your job outlook is not too stable, or you'll need substantial amounts for improvements to the house, it would seem wiser to assume less for (1) than your forecast suggests. Weigh the situation carefully—it's a very important decision.

When you do get to look at an apartment, look at the entire building as well. Its overall appearance will give you a clue about the upkeep and the condition of the structure. Inquire about the tenants already living there. Are there children, teenagers, or noisy adults? Is there garage space available? Does this cost extra and is it safe? Are any rental increases anticipated? Is the rent controlled or stabilized? What kind of lease is there, month-to-month or long term? Are utilities included or extra? How often is the apartment redecorated? Who pays for this? If you have used a real estate broker to find an apartment, you may be expected to pay a percentage of the year's rent or one or more months' rent as a brokerage fee. Generally at least one extra month's rent in addition to the first month is expected as a down payment. Deposits for telephone and electric service are usual in most large cities also. Read and re-read all leases or agreements before signing, and have your attorney explain anything that you might not understand. Know what you are signing. Many of the previously mentioned precautions in joint ownership also apply to a joint rental arrangement. You don't want to be left "holding the bag" if your roommate unexpectedly moves out.

SUMMARY

There are, of course, other options for a home not mentioned in this chapter. Mobile homes have become much more popular recently and have several advantages and disadvantages, particularly if they are truly mobile homes. People also still build homes themselves, or live in government or institutional housing. If your home, however, is not only where your heart is, but also your money, then it is either an investment or a consumption cost. As an investment it can be an exceptionally good one.

11 Investing in Stocks and Bonds

Dorothy J. del Bueno

BASIC INFORMATION ABOUT STOCKS

WHEN YOU buy a share of stock you buy ownership in the issuing corporation. Stocks, unlike bonds, are equity in the company. Owning part of the company entitles you to share in the profits of the business, to vote in the election of directors and to participate in other decisions as determined to be part of the stockholders meeting. You don't have to attend the meeting to cast your vote, but can vote by mail or proxy. Owning stock in a company also gives you a lien on the assets if the company should fail. Preferred stockholders take precedence over common stockholders, however. That's why they are called preferred. (Bond holders come even before preferred stockholders!)

The principal advantages of stocks as an investment are that they are relatively easy to liquidate or convert into cash, and that their value is being continuously monitored. The goal in purchasing stock is to obtain a profit equal to or greater than the loss in the purchasing power of the dollar because of inflation and taxation. Obviously, this goal will only be met if the value of the stock goes up! When you invest in stocks you are taking a risk that the company will do well, turn a profit, and therefore increase the value of the stock.

Reading a Stock Quotation

It is relatively easy to find out how major stocks are doing. Most daily urban newspapers provide information on stocks listed on the New York Stock Exchange (NYSE) or "big board," and the American Stock Exchange (AMEX). The NYSE is composed of over 1,300 members who buy a "seat" on the exchange. These members represent brokerage firms whose primary business is buying and selling securities. To be listed on the NYSE, a company must meet very stringent standards related to earnings, assets, number of shares outstanding, and number of stockholders. The Amex represents primarily younger and smaller companies.

A stock listing looks like this:

72   62   Grand Goods   1.25   12   72   63⅛   59¾   62   1⅛

What do all these symbols and numbers mean? The first number indicates the highest price paid for the stock this year. In the example, the high was 72, or $72.00 per share. The second number indicates the lowest price paid per share for the stock during the year to date. In the example, the low was $62.00 per share. Next is the name of the company the stock represents. In the example, Grand Goods is the name of the company. Often the name will be represented by a set of letters or abbreviations such as ATT (American Telephone and Telegraph), or Gen Elec (General Electric). The company may be listed more than once with letters or symbols following the name. These indicate different issues of stock such as preferred or convertible preferred.

The next figure indicates the annual dividend paid by the stock. The dividend figure is an estimate based on the last dividend paid. In the example, 1.25 indicates that an estimated dividend value of $1.25 per share is anticipated. The figure 12 in the example given represents the Price Earnings Ratio (P/E), which gives an indication of investors' perception of the value of the stock. The P/E Ratio is calculated by dividing the twelve month earnings into the price of the stock. For example, if the stock is selling at $100.00 per share and the earnings over the last twelve months were $10.00, the stock has a P/E ratio of 10, meaning an investor is paying ten dollars for one dollar of earnings. Our stock, Grand Goods has a P/E Ratio of twelve, meaning it will take twelve dollars of investment to get one dollar of earnings. Price earnings ratios vary greatly from industry to industry but are often similar within industries such as chemical or steel companies. Growth industries may have higher P/E ratios than established industries. Remember, however, that the P/E ratio is based on last year's earnings. This year may be very different, so keep this information in perspective and try to determine what the company will do in the future.

The next number given in the listing, 72 in our example, indicates the number of shares of the stock traded for the day, expressed in lots of one hundred. Seven thousand two hundred shares of Grand Goods were traded, bought or sold, in yesterday's market. 63⅛ and 59¾ represent the highest and lowest price paid for a share of stock on the previous trading day. Grand Goods' high for the day was sixty three dollars and twelve and a half cents per share. (Parts of a dollar are expressed in eighths, quarters and halves) The lowest price paid in the previous day's trading was fifty nine dollars and seventy five cents. The closing price, the next to the last figure in the listing, was sixty-two dollars per share. The final figure in the stock listing is the net change, or the difference between the closing price of the last sale on this day's trading and the closing price of the previous trading day. For Grand Goods there was a net change or difference of a loss of one dollar and twelve and a half cents (−1⅛) per share.

If a stock in which you are interested is not listed on either the NYSE or the Amex, it may be either because the stock is not popular or it is an "over-the-counter" stock. The over-the-counter market represents stocks that are not listed on any exchange but are traded by brokers through private negotiation. The volume of over-the-counter stocks is much greater than that of the exchange securities. Over-the-counter stocks represent all types of companies and businesses, both speculative and conservative. Information on unlisted stocks can be obtained from a broker or investment service.

Although it is easy to read a stock listing it is difficult to make consistently good decisions. The market price of a stock reflects the opinions of those people who are buying and selling as well as the performance of the company behind the stock. There are trends and fashions even in the stock market. Subjective factors, and timing can also affect what happens. Even the experts aren't always right!

Stock Market Jargon and Terms

Dividends. Dividends are the earnings or profits of the corporation paid out to the share-holders. All earnings or profits are not necessarily paid out as dividends, however. A corporation can retain

100% of the profits or earnings for research and development, expansion, or any other reason. Dividends on preferred stock are usually a fixed amount per share and are a priority over common stock dividends. Common stock dividends may also be a fixed amount, such as a dollar per share, but can be eliminated, increased, decreased, or paid more than once during the year as an extra dividend. The yield of the stock is determined by dividing the price of the stock into the dividend. For example, our Grand Goods stock cost $62.00 per share and paid an estimated dividend of $1.25. This is a yield of 2%; not a real winner! Dividends on common stock are, unlike savings account interest, tax free up to a specified dollar value. Therefore, stock dividends have an advantage over the higher savings account interest.

Buying and Selling.   Although it is relatively simple to trade stocks, it is not exactly the same as buying groceries! First, you need to establish an account or credit line with a broker or a bank who will do the trading for you. Shop around! Select a broker who has a credible reputation, reasonable charges, and who can provide you with the investment services you need to meet your objectives. Most brokers will both implement your orders and provide you with information and advice. A "market order" tells the broker to buy or sell the stock at its trading price or last sale price. A "stop-order" tells the broker to buy or sell a stock at a given price. When the price reaches the specified price, the stock is traded. If the stock does not reach the specified price the order is not executed. You will be expected to pay for purchase orders promptly and in full. Usually, you will also receive a monthly statement of your account. The stock you purchase may be held by the broker or delivered to you. Obviously, to sell stock you must turn the stock certificates over to the broker. If you keep the stock certificates yourself be sure to keep them in a safe or safety deposit box. Although the certificates are registered in your name, it is still smart to protect them from theft or destruction.

Commissions are the fees you pay to a broker or bank to implement your trading orders. The commission may be fixed, i.e., so much per share, a flat fee, or variable depending on the size of the transaction. It generally costs more in commissions to buy small amounts or odd lots (less than 100 shares) of stock. When you are determining the return on investment of your stock, you should include the cost of trading the security as part of the purchase price.

As with any other purchase today, it is possible to buy stock on credit, or as it is called in the trade, on margin. The Federal Reserve Board sets margin requirements that outline the "rules of the road." The margin requirement specifies how much can be "charged," in what period the balance charged must be paid, and what kind and amount of collateral can be used to back your credit. You also pay interest for the use of the credit extended. Buying on margin is generally not a good idea for the novice or unsophisticated investor.

Stockholders are sometimes offered the opportunity to buy rights and options. A specified number of rights entitles the owner to purchase within a certain time limit additional shares of stock at a price that may be lower than the market price of the stock. Options are contractual agreements that give the option owner the opportunity to buy or sell stock at a specified price within an established time period. Options to buy are "call options" and options to sell are "put options." Rights and options can also be bought and sold on the market.

"Blue Chips" and Growth Stocks.   Stocks that are considered high value because of their consistent earning performance and payment of dividends are sometimes referred to as "blue chip" stocks. These stocks are considered to be a low risk investment because of their proven record and favorable future. However, nothing is a sure thing in the stock market and even a blue chip can decline in value.

Growth stocks represent companies that have shown growth in the past and are predicted to show increase in value in the future even if the economy or other similar companies don't do well. Growth companies are ordinarily the recognized leaders in the field, the dominant company, the emerging front runners, or the innovators.

Investing in blue chips or growth stocks may be one way to protect your investment. Another method to protect your investment is to do business with a broker who is a member of the Securities Investor Protection Corporation (SIPC). The SIPC is a non-government corporation that provides financial protection similar to that provided for savings investments by the FDIC (Federal Deposit Insurance Corporation). The SIPC protects registered or about-to-be-registered securities held by member brokers. Should the broker be in danger of failure your securities are protected up to a maximum of $100,000.

There is, however, no insurance protection for the loss of

your investment because no one is willing to pay the price asked or because the market "falls." This is the risk you assume in purchasing stocks.

Tips from the Experts

1.   Don't Listen to Tips.   How many times have you heard about a hot stock from your hairdresser or garageman who has a friend in the "know." If your hairdresser is so smart, why is she still doing hair? Stick to active, seasoned stock issues that are listed on major stock exchanges and use a reputable broker for advice or suggestions.

2.   Watch Your Stock!   Timing is important in the stock market. You want to buy when the stock is on the way up and sell when it's on the way down. Price is important, but only in relation to what will happen to the price. If a stock is $2.00 a share, it's only a good investment if it goes up. A $100.00 a share stock may be better if it will go to $150.00. You must be willing to spend time following the progress of your stock. Remember, it is generally easier psychologically to buy than to sell. Human greed makes us want to make more by waiting. Don't be afraid to sell and minimize your losses.

3.   Do Your Homework!   You can learn about your anticipated stock investment by getting fact sheets from your broker or directly from Standard and Poor. Annual Reports are also available from companies. You can learn more about the stock market, its hazards and benefits by taking courses offered by brokerage houses, community colleges, and institutes. You can read the financial journals such as *Barrons,* the *Wall Street Journal,* or *Forbes.* There are also numerous books and pamphlets published each year to help you become more knowledgeable.

4.   Know What You Want!   Stocks are generally considered an investment for appreciation or increase in value of capital. A stock that pays a substantial dividend but increases little in price is probably not as good an investment as one that has no dividend but doubles in price. Determine how much you can afford to risk and how much you will need to invest to increase your capital and protect its purchasing power. Make a commitment to that risk. One way to take a plunge in the stock market with only a minimal amount of money is to join an investment club. Individual members of the club pool small sums of money to buy and sell selected stocks. Members usually meet to discuss and analyze, with the help of a broker, what stocks to trade. There is also a National Association of Investment Clubs which can provide you with more information. Their address is 1515 East Eleven Mile Road, Royal Oak, Michigan 48068.

5. *Remember Death and Taxes — Both Are Inevitable.* Although there is no way to avoid death, taxes are another matter. You probably can't avoid them completely either, but you can certainly try to use the tax laws legally to your advantage. Capital gains from stock transactions are subject to taxation. Dividends from stocks are not (up to a specific dollar amount). Chapter 13 tells you more about taxes and what to do about them.

What happens in the stock market is not only based on logic and objective criteria such as annual reports and profit and loss statements. Emotional reactions, hopes, fears, and acts of God often influence the market. Stock investments are not for the timid or faint hearted. Be prepared for the worst and work for the best!

HOW ABOUT BONDS?

Bonds are generally considered a more conservative investment than stocks. A bond holder is a creditor of the issuing agency, not an owner. A bond holder makes a loan to the bond issuer who in turn promises to pay the owner of the bond a guaranteed rate of interest for the period of time until the debt is paid off. Bond holders have preference over stock holders in the event of the liquidation of assets. The chief disadvantage of bonds is that they cannot increase in value over the established or face amount of the bond. Bonds provide guaranteed income but minimal capital gains. What are other differences between stocks and bonds? Bond holders must pay taxes on interest from bonds unless they are the tax exempt variety. It generally costs less to purchase bonds but it is difficult to invest sums less than $5000.00, unless you join a fund of some kind.

Bonds are less speculative than stocks because the principal is safe if you can afford to wait until maturity or until the bond is paid off. The income or interest is guaranteed and the yield is generally greater than for common stocks. However, as already indicated, there is less opportunity for capital appreciation. Bonds are considered to be excellent collateral since their face value is guaranteed if held to maturity. Speculative risk can also be minimized by investing in bonds with ratings of A or better.

Buying and Selling

The bond market is much larger than the stock market and is more an institutional than an individual market. Bonds, generally traded over-the-counter, are issued in denominations of $1000.00 or more. This face value is the amount that will be paid on maturity of the bond. Bonds are listed, however, with the last digit dropped. For example, if the bond is selling at $950.00 it will be listed as 95. If the bond is selling at greater than its face value it is designated at "a premium," if selling at less than face value, it is designated at "a discount." The selling price of a bond is generally inversely related to interest rates. As interest rates rise, prices tend to fall because buyers would rather buy a new bond with a higher interest rate than an old bond with a lower interest rate.

The length of issue or maturity date of bonds may be short or long. Twenty or thirty year maturity dates are common. The bond issuer has the right, however, to pay off or redeem the bond before the established maturity date. This is termed "calling" the bond. The call date, or earliest date the bond can be redeemed, and the price at which it will be called are both specified.

As already stated, the interest rate on bonds is fixed. Interest rates on bonds have increased considerably over the last ten years. What the future will hold is any one's guess. Interest rates today are like yo-yo's. They keep going up and down. Some of the factors affecting interest rates are the demand for money, the availability of money, the prime rate or what banks charge their best customers, federal funds rates or what banks charge one another, and the Federal Reserve System. There are no simple formulas to predict interest rates.

The price you pay for a bond is inversely related to the current yield, or the relationship between the interest rate and selling price. For example, if you pay $10,000 for a bond that has a face value of $10,000 and the interest is 8%, the current yield will be 8%. If you pay $9,000 for that same bond, the yield would be 8.9%. If you paid $11,000 for the bond the yield would be 7.27%. The yield to maturity, or what you make if you hold the bond to maturity is more difficult to calculate because you must include interest plus profit or loss at maturity. There are standard tables for yield to maturity. Your broker can help you with this computation.

Bonds are rated according to their degree or risk. The rating is done by several organizations; Standard and Poor, Moody's, and Fitch. The top ratings start at AAA (triple A) and go down to D or

D—. High rated bonds are low risk bonds. Although the different rating institutions use somewhat different abbreviations, their ratings are similar and consistent. Ratings are renewed annually and can change. Bonds with high ratings and low risk will usually have lower interest rates than low rating bonds. Obviously, the purchaser must have some incentive for taking the risk. U.S. Treasury and other federal government agency bonds are usually not rated because they are considered very low risk.

Bonds can be registered or bearer bonds. Bearer bonds are owned by the person who has possession of them. They are easier to trade than registered bonds, but must be rigorously safeguarded because ownership is not registered. Bearer bonds usually include coupons for the interest payment. These coupons are clipped and sent for payment at the owner's discretion. The interest on registered bonds is sent by mail to the bond owner at designated intervals.

Types of Bonds

There are many different types of bonds that are issued each year. Debentures are bonds that are issued without collateral. Corporate bonds are issued by private corporations and come with a wide variety of interest rates, maturity periods, and ratings. There are bonds called convertibles that can be exchanged into a specific number of shares of common stock. These are considered more speculative than ordinary bonds because of their wide price fluctuation.

The United States Treasury issues many types of bonds as well as bills and notes. Any debt issued by the United States Government is considered to be highly liquid, very low risk, and usually provides attractive yields. U.S. Government issues are also free from municipal and state taxation.

Treasury Bills. Two sets of bills are issued every week, one set maturing in 91 days and the other set maturing in 182 days. Also, on a monthly basis, two additional bills with nine month and one year maturity dates respectively are issued. There is no stated rate of interest on treasury bills. The interest is the difference between the face value and selling price. The minimum denomination is $10,000.00 and they can be purchased at Federal Reserve Banks or its branches.

Treasury Notes. These usually carry a maturity period of from one to seven years and a fixed rate of interest. Notes come in denominations of $1,000 or more and are purchased from Federal Reserve Banks, bond brokers, or commercial banks.

Treasury Bonds. These come in many different series, the most familiar being Series E, or savings bonds. Treasury bonds may be subject to call, have both a fixed maturity date and rate of interest, and are both of the bearer and registered type. The rate of return on most of the series is not as good as on other types of bonds.

Other federal agencies as well as states and municipalities also offer bonds to institutional and individual investors. "Municipals" have become, in the past few years, of much greater interest to the individual investor, primarily because of their exemption from federal taxes and state taxes when purchased in the state of origin. Municipals generally carry lower rates of interest than corporates, are coupon bearer bonds, are sold in large denominations, and are rated lower or not rated at all. There are many types of municipals based on the revenue source that is allocated for payback. It is particularly important to get expert advice and analysis of risk before investing in municipal bonds.

Helpful Hints

It is probably obvious to you by now that the bond market is confusing and even more complex than the stock market. Some guidelines recommended by the experts are:

1. Shop around and deal only with credible brokers or investment departments that have established track records and reputations.
2. Only buy bonds of top quality such as the federal government issues or bonds rated AA or better.
3. Buy new issues and avoid bonds close to call date or subject to early call.
4. Review your portfolio at least yearly.

A WORD ABOUT FUNDS

Funds or pools, although established in 1920, are a fairly recent phenomenon for most investors. The investor in a bond fund buys a portion of the portfolio of bonds and securities owned by the fund. There are many types of funds, all with different features. Some funds charge a sales charge on purchases and are called "load" funds. Some do not charge a sales charge but do charge commissions. Some funds are called no-load or no charge. Mutual or open-end funds continuously buy and sell shares in the fund to the public. The shares are sold at a specific but fluctuating value. Closed-end funds or publically traded investment funds are purchased in the over-the-counter market and may be purchased at a discount or premium. Unit trusts have limited membership, make one-time sales of the units that carry a face value, accrued interest, and sales charge, and have a fixed portfolio. There are many other types of funds. As a potential investor you should become familiar with their features before making a decision of choice. In general the advantages of funds are: Diversification of securities within the fund, professional management, relative safety because of diversification and federal regulation, liquidity, and convenience (someone else is taking care of the details). The disadvantages of funds are the lack of personal choice in selection of the securities in the fund portfolio, sales charges or commissions may erode the return on your investment, and the difficulty in evaluating or comparing funds because of the plethora of choices.

Investing in stocks or bonds can be exciting and financially rewarding. It can also be anxiety producing and disastrous. Which adjectives will be descriptive of your experience depends a lot on how well informed you are in your choices and a little good luck shouldn't hurt either!

12 Insurance and Pension Funds

J. R. Salisbury

Statistically it's been shown that women are buying more and more life insurance with every passing year. Perhaps this is due to the fact that there are now more working women, proportionately, than ever before. Many women have families at home for whom they want to provide if anything happens to them. Women today have been made much more aware of financial matters and responsibilities. What once was thought of as almost exclusively a man's province is no longer the case. For instance, when a woman's salary is counted in the family budget, the loss of her portion of the household income would be severely felt and is, therefore, highly insurable. A career or single woman who has elected not to marry needs to provide for her future security. If a woman is the sole support of a family, her safeguards must be the same as a man's. The average financial contribution made to a family by a wife and mother is estimated today at well over $11,000 per year. This value should be guaranteed in the case of her disability or death.

If you fall into the family responsibility category, it would be wise to make a rough estimate of the income your family would need after your death. Evaluate what they could receive from salaries, dividends, interest, social security and any other sources. The difference between available income and needed income is the amount that should be covered by life insurance. As with most matters of personal finance and investment, the safest thing to do is to seek advice, in this case, that of a qualified insurance agent. Using the recommendation of a trusted friend is a good approach. You can also contact the National Association of Life Underwriters, who will in turn refer you to a reputable agent. The agent can help you correlate what you need with what you can afford.

LIFE INSURANCE

There are three basic types of life insurance: whole life, term, and endowment.

Whole Life. The ordinary life plan offers a level death benefit no matter at what age death occurs. It requires a uniform premium amount throughout the insured's (and the policy's) lifetime. The normal chance of death increases with age, of course, and accordingly the premium for a level amount of life insurance coverage would be expected to increase yearly as well, until in old age the annual premium would grow to a prohibitive amount. However, with this plan, you pay more during the early years of your policy, thus paying less later when your income may be substantially reduced.

Generally, women live longer than men. Therefore, their premiums are usually lower — a most equitable arrangement! You may cash in this type of policy or borrow against its value. Whole life plans are somewhat flexible and can be altered if insurance needs change.

Term Insurance. Term plans differ from whole life in that they provide protection for a specific period or term. At the end of the specified term the policy expires. At this time you may be able to renew the policy. The limited time period of coverage is usually specified as so many years or to a specific age. If renewed for an additional time period, the premiums are higher based on the insured person's current age. Term insurance offers little, if any, cash value. Many policies of this sort may be converted to whole life any time during the term period without proof of insurability, that is, without medical examination.

Simplified examples of these two plans follow.

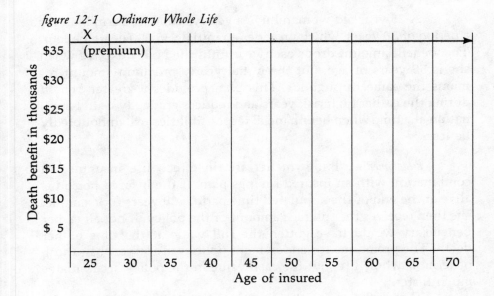

figure 12-1   *Ordinary Whole Life*

A 25 year old woman selects a plan whereby she is provided with a $35,000 death benefit, and pays a fixed premium of "X" dollars per year. Both the amount of the benefit and the premium will remain level for life.

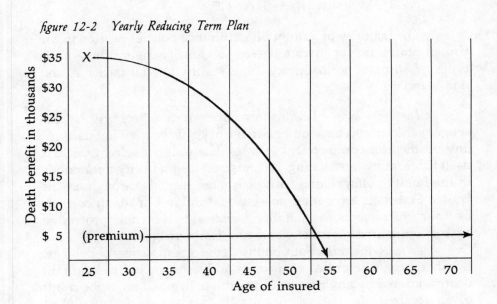

figure 12-2   *Yearly Reducing Term Plan*

A 25 year old woman buys a yearly reducing Term Plan for a period of 30 years, which provides an initial $35,000 death benefit. This benefit amount drops each year until the policy expires when she is 55 years of age, but the initial yearly premium amount remains the same throughout. This plan provides a greater benefit during the earlier high risk years and reduces gradually until termination at a time when her financial responsibilities will undoubtedly be less.

Endowments.   Endowments are, in effect, life insurance in combination with an insured savings plan. If the insured person is alive at the end of the stipulated time period, 30 years for example, she then receives the full face amount of the policy. If not alive, her beneficiary would have gotten the full value at the time of her death. The premiums for endowment policies are larger than those of term or whole life, but the cash value in the policy accumulates much faster.

There are many variations and possibilities in these types of plans. Consultation with a well informed insurance specialist will help you obtain the advice needed to select the life insurance program best suited to your own needs.

AUTOMOBILE INSURANCE

The majority of automobile insurance policies written in the United States are for private passenger cars. There are three basic types of automobile insurance: family auto, special package, and non-standard.

The family auto   classification covers four-wheel private passenger vehicles and pick-up or panel trucks, if they are not used for any business or commercial purposes. If a four-wheeled vehicle is used for farming or ranching, it is referred to as a utility automobile in the family policy. Family auto coverage extends throughout the United States, its territories, possessions, and in Canada. It consists of four main sections: liability, medical payments, protection against uninsured motorists, and physical damage.

Liability includes both bodily damage and property damage. Bodily injury is described as sickness or disease, including resultant death, suffered by any person during the policy period, as the result of an accident. Property damage is the damage or destruction of property, including loss of use.

Medical payments provides for payment of all reasonable medical and dental expenses incurred by the insured or a relative residing with him, while occupying an owned auto, a non-owned auto being used with the owner's permission, or through being struck by an automobile. In about half of our states, this "medical payment" has been replaced by "No-Fault" coverage, providing certain benefits to injured persons in an auto accident regardless of liability (fault). Some no-fault laws provide only limited benefits, while others are without dollar limitation.

Protection against uninsured motorists. In most states only body injury is covered, paying all sums the insured and his resident relatives are legally entitled to recover as damages from the owner or driver of an uninsured automobile in an accident, or by a hit-and-run driver.

Physical damage covers damage or destruction of the insured's own car, and is an optional part of the policy. It may include the following items.

"Comprehensive." This pays for almost any loss or damage to the owned car (or a non-owned car driven with permission) **except** loss by collision with another object, or by upset of the automobile. Among other coverages included are loss from: explosion, windstorm, hail, vandalism, falling objects, breakage of glass and an almost unlimited list of others! Comprehensive also includes loss of personal effects from the insured owner's car.

"Collision." This covers loss or damage to the insured auto from collision with another object or by upset of the car. This is almost always written along with Comprehensive coverage, and usually includes a deductible amount of, for example, $100 or $200. This means that the insured individual pays the first $100 or $200 of a loss, and the company covers the balance.

"Towing and labor." This may be an optional coverage with a limit of $25 per service call for towing the insured's auto or a borrowed private car, or for labor performed at the place of disablement.

Special Package Insurance is preferred risk, lower rate auto insurance available with some variations in almost every state for the better-than-average-risk. Of necessity there are many limitations governing eligibility. Special package insurance is usually written in two parts. First, liability, medical expense (or no-fault), accidental death benefit and protection against uninsured motorists and, second, comprehensive and collision. If you think you qualify for this kind of auto insurance consult your insurance agent.

Non-Standard Insurance   provides the same basic coverage as the Family Auto Policy, but is for those who find it difficult to obtain private passenger insurance. Reasons for this difficulty may be any of the following: The applicant (or any operator) has had auto insurance cancelled or renewal refused; An operator has been convicted in the previous three years of operating a car under the influence of drugs or alcohol; The vehicle to be insured is a sports car and is operated by an individual not having a good driving record for the past five years; The operator is required to file evidence of financial responsibility for reasons other than age. Non-standard insurance is surcharged 35%, 50%, or 75%, based on certain standards which may vary from state to state.

There are any number of endorsements available as additions to or extensions of various policies, usually at additional cost. An applicant who may not be able to meet requirements for auto insurance because of age or a poor driving record, may still secure coverage through the "Assigned Risk Plan," usually operated by the state. The Assigned Risk Plan is basically an agreement among auto insurance companies operating in that state to take uninsurable individuals as risks. Each company assumes a percentage of these risks in proportion to the amount of business the company writes in that state.

All insurance premiums are determined basically by location. In the case of private passenger autos, premiums are determined by how and by whom the auto is used. Currently, in all fifty states, there are Financial Responsibility Laws or Compulsory Insurance Laws requiring that owners or operators lose their licenses if they cannot meet their responsibilities for accidents and/or judgments to the limit provided by law. An individual may furnish evidence of financial dependability with cash, with a bond, or with an insurance policy.

FIRE AND THEFT INSURANCE

Every insurance policy will enumerate the obligations of both the insured and the company if a loss occurs. There must be cooperation between the insured and his company. An understanding of your policy and its contents will facilitate such cooperation. After you've made arrangements with an agent to handle your insurance account, go over his suggestions thoroughly. Do the same thing with the final policies when you receive them. If you have questions of any sort, contact the agent at once, preferably in writing, for an explanation.

What should you look for in fire and theft insurance? A home and its possessions naturally mean a great deal to everyone, but all too often are taken for granted and not properly safeguarded. The so called "Homeowner" policy, in six basic forms, is the most concise type of protection you can select. Generally the forms are the following.

1. Property loss caused by fire, smoke, lightning, windstorm, hail, vehicles, vandalism or malicious mischief, theft, breakage of glass, personal liability including medical payments, physical damage you may cause to the property of others, and defense against lawsuits. This is an adequate type of policy for young families who own small homes and for older people who live on reduced incomes. It is the most reasonable of the Homeowner Policies.

2. Includes all the coverages of the above, plus water damage from faulty appliances, freezing of plumbing systems, weight of ice and snow, damages from owned vehicles, riot and civil commotion, and theft on or off the premises.

3. Includes all of the above, as well as more comprehensive coverage. It is the most widely recommended as the best protection for the money for homeowners having well-maintained property of substantial value.

4. This policy is for tenants of a dwelling and parallels #2, above, with the major exception of the dwelling itself.

5. "All-Risk" coverage is designed for families who want the broadest coverage available. It is the most expensive type of homeowners policy.

6. Condominium owners' insurance provides coverage for the personal property and activities of the condo unit owner. It is similar to insurance provided an apartment tenant, but is designed to overlap with insurance carried by a Condominium Association for the common risks of all the unit owners.

Any items of special value are protected only up to certain limits on any homeowners policy. For example, jewelry and furs, silverware, coins, stamp collections and cameras may require a special "floater" policy to provide the extra coverage needed. In some areas of the country you may not be able to get theft insurance at all on certain items because of high crime rates. Numerous endorsements can also be added to any of these policies to tailor them to your particular needs. An additional premium is usually charged for special requirements.

ACCIDENT AND HEALTH INSURANCE

As you might expect, accident insurance provides for the expenses incurred when an accident takes place. If you're injured on the job, your employer will provide, through Workers' Compensation, medical insurance as well as weekly income if the injury is serious. Nonwork related accidents also can cause lost time and huge medical bills. Accident policies provide the necessary coverage to fill this need. They are usually written with a specific limit or Principle Sum which is paid if death occurs or total permanent disability results. Accident policies usually pay one-half of the policy limit if there is loss of a limb or an eye. In the case of such a loss, these monies can be used to help in vocational readjustment.

The purpose of health or hospitalization insurance is also obvious. In its basic form, health insurance covers illness that requires hospitalization. It may also be expanded to cover outpatient expenses, dental bills, eye examinations and other needs. If coverage is provided by your employer, a booklet will be provided that outlines the specific benefits. A self-employed person should look for coverage in three basic areas; hospitalization, surgery, and major medical. For the first two items there are usually time limits and dollar limits. In cases of serious or extended illness, these limits may be reached rapidly. Major medical coverage is then used. It usually pays for 80% of these extended expenses up to the policy limit. Major medical premiums are usually not too expensive as most hospital stays are of short duration. When needed, however, it is definitely worth its price.

DISABILITY INSURANCE

Perhaps the single most important form of insurance to carry is disability coverage. Disability insurance replaces income if you become ill or disabled, a time when financial loss is a crucial blow.

Disability insurance is exceedingly important if you're the head of a household (even a household of one!). It is frequently offered to employees by their employer and is a most reasonable way to assure yourself of a very necessary protection. If unavailable through your employer, or if you're self-employed, contact your agent without delay to discuss this vital form of insurance. The American Nurses' Association also offers its members Disability Insurance at reasonable rates. Policies vary from one insurance company to the next, but each will contain certain basic fundamental provisions. The most important feature is income protection in case of disability. In insurance jargon this means "the inability of an insured to perform an occupation as a result of either sickness or accidental injury." A monthly amount is paid to the insured to replace her regular income. This monthly benefit continues, in most cases for the period specified in the policy, or until age sixty-five, whichever is less. Sickness benefits, however, usually cover benefits for five years, and in some instances to age sixty-five. There is a waiting period after the injury or sickness prior to commencement of payments. The minimum waiting period is seven days. This avoids claims for minor accidental injuries and for non-serious illnesses such as colds! The insured will have a choice of several lengths of waiting periods. The cost of the insurance premiums is related to the length of the waiting period.

There is partial disability insurance available also. It is purchased as an additional provision and pays monthly one-half of the total disability payments (for up to six months) following a period of total disability.

Make sure that the policy you are considering allows for a rehabilitation period, is renewable, and is non-cancelable. Premiums are established according to the occupational classification of the applicant. It stands to reason that some hazardous occupations will carry a greater chance for injury or sickness. Also, these hazardous job classifications may affect the period of total disability. An insured person doing manual work might not be able to return to the job as soon as a disabled office employee. Certain groups of applicants may also be required to have physical exams before coverage can be written.

Most people who have ever been formally employed also qualify for disability benefits under the Social Security program and, in addition, most states have a form of Workmen's Compensation Insurance. These plans are generally not sufficient to cover your needs. They will, however, serve as a basis for determining how much additional disability insurance you will want or need. Keep in mind that an individual under the age of sixty-five is more likely to become disabled or suffer a prolonged illness than to die!

The previous paragraphs have briefly described the subject of insurance. There are a vast number of additional types of coverage. We can't emphasize strongly enough that you should find an insurance specialist or general agent for advice and counsel in regard to obtaining the optional coverage your pocketbook will allow!

RETIREMENT AND PENSION PLANS

Selecting the most favorable program to prepare for your retirement years is a complex matter, but well worth giving time and thought to at the very beginning of your career. Of course our federal Social Security plan is a retirement plan, but most people aspire to and reach a standard of living considerably above the level that social security benefits will offer. A satisfactory retirement income should be greater than half of the income earned during the working years. That amount, considering reduced needs and taxes, should be adequate to provide for the basic necessities of life. A retirement plan, adequately prepared, will provide you with peace of mind that your future is taken care of. You can then give attention to your present responsibilities — and pleasures!

A qualified retirement plan, that is one that meets certain government requirements, benefits both employer and employee. The Federal Government encourages employers to help their employees build sufficient retirement incomes by giving extremely favorable income tax treatment to qualified retirement plans. What are some of the tax advantages?

Contributions made by the employer to a participating employee's pension fund are not taxable until the retirement benefits begin, when the employee's income (and therefore tax bracket) is likely to be much lower. Generally, income on the funds' investments is accummulated on an income tax-free basis, enabling the fund to grow much larger than if annual earnings were subject to income taxes. This is an important advantage of a qualified plan. When an employee's death benefit under a qualified plan is paid as an annuity to a beneficiary other than to the employee's estate, it is then not subject to federal estate tax, enabling the beneficiary to receive such death benefits in full.

Following are three possible programs that may be applicable in your personal situation:

The Keogh Plan

Legislation enacted by the United States Government in 1962 created the "Self Employed Individuals Tax Retirement Act," popularly known as the Keogh Act after the man who guided it through Congress. This act opened a much broader market for personal pension plans than was formerly available. Those participating individuals may now enjoy tax-favored savings in planning for their retirement. Some of the same principles apply as do under qualified corporate pension plans, for Congress has stated that self-employed persons must be treated (for qualified retirement plan purposes) partly as employers (of themselves) and partly as employees.

As employers, the self-employed are permitted to deduct contributions made to pension plans for their own benefits. As with employees, they are not taxed currently on part of such contributions made for their benefit, or on the income earned under the plan during the accumulation period, but are taxed when the benefits are received.

Any employee covered under a Keogh Plan is entitled to his benefits even though employment might be terminated. Should termination occur the payment of those benefits may be postponed until normal retirement date. The amount permitted to be contributed in one's own behalf to a Keogh Plan is determined by "earned income," and is limited to 15% of earned income or $7500 (whichever is less) annually.

There are exceptions to many of the foregoing regulations, but keep in mind that this chapter is intented merely to acquaint you with the basic facts. Refinements of these (and other) plans must be carefully explored, preferably with the aid of your bank or a knowledgeable insurance advisor.

IRA Plan

As of 1974, under the "Employment Retirement Income Security Act," any wage earner who is self-employed but not a proprietor or in partnership can arrange for his or her own individual retirement account. This plan is commonly called an IRA. It is similar to the Keogh Plan but not limited to self-employed proprietors or partners and their employees, as previously mentioned.

Under government regulation, it allows up to 15% of your salary (to a maximum of $1500 yearly) to be invested in a bank, insurance company, the stock market or certain government investments. You may then take a tax deduction for your yearly amount, deferring tax until you receive the benefits, and interest credited tax free. The total sum cannot be available to you until you reach the age of at least fifty-nine and a half years, without paying immediate tax at the rate of 6%, and it must be withdrawn no later than the age of seventy and one half years. This IRA plan is **not** available if any other retirement plan is offered through the employee's company, or if a Keogh Plan, certain federal or state government employee plans, some public school teachers' plans, etc. are used. It is simply to provide for those individuals having no pension possibilities.

A popular IRA program is the Tax Deferred Annuity (T.D.A.), providing fixed investments for guaranteed interest, or common stock investments used as a hedge against inflation, or a combination of these. The accumulated funds may be used to provide monthly annuity payments at retirement for as long as you live, or may be surrendered for cash whenever you wish. Specifically designed for school system employees, hospitals and certain other non-profit organizations, it can only be offered through life insurance companies. Your salary is reduced by the amount you elect to contribute to the plan. This amount is tax free and is limited to approximately 20% of salary for a new employee in your job. This amount is then invested in a broad portfolio of common stocks (variable annuity), or in fixed assets such as mortgages and bonds (fixed-dollar annuity). Following retirement, your monthly annuity payments fluctuate with the variable annuity in accordance with the stock market. The fixed-dollar annuity guarantees each payment at the same rate. A combination of these plans may be selected. With each contribution you receive a statement and a year-end summary showing the status of your account. This tax deferred annuity will not affect any other retirement plans you may have. For example: You're in a 25% tax bracket, and have elected to set aside $1200 yearly.

Without tax deferral		*With tax deferral*
$1200	Set aside from salary	$1200
$ 300	Tax Paid	$ 000
$ 900	Net Dollars Set Aside	$1200

With $300 working for you which you would ordinarily have paid in taxes, your actual cost is only $900. The $1200 is set aside for your retirement.

Corporate Plans

There are essentially three types of employer (corporate) pension plans available. The profit sharing plan says, in effect, that if the company makes a profit each year it will set aside money for each employee's retirement in a trust fund. However, without a profit, they are not obliged to do so.

In a defined contribution plan a commitment is made by the employer to put aside a certain percentage of each person's pay each year, with the eventual takeout sum remaining unknown. Most labor union plans are of this type.

The defined benefit plan is the opposite of the defined contribution plan. What you'll receive (the benefit) is what you know. The unknown factor is the amount of the contributions.

If you are working and are eligible for a pension plan you should ask the following questions. When am I eligible? (Sometimes 25 years of age and one year of service is required before eligibility). What is the vesting schedule? (Vesting refers to the amount that cannot be taken away from the individual covered.) The schedule for vesting varies, but cannot by law be longer than fifteen years in any plan.

When is retirement possible? What is the usual retirement age? What is the earliest age at which I can retire? Is there any penalty for earlier retirement? Do I pay for any portion of the pension? If so, is that portion I contribute fully vested? Has the company informed me fully about the plan? (The law states that the employer must give a booklet in easily understood language to the employee. A statement giving estimates of your retirement benefits, your vested benefits, and any changes occurring during the year must also be given. The name of the Plan Administrator must also be included.)

In taking your pension upon retirement, there are four general options open to you:

1. A lump sum (not a good choice, for your money will be taxed in its entirety that year.)
2. Various annuities (paid in monthly installments). This is particularly good for a single person.

3. Life annuity with ten years "certain" (paid as long as you live, but not less than ten years).
4. Joint ½ survivor annuity (X number of dollars for as long as you live and half that amount for as long as your survivor lives.)

As a final suggestion and word of advice, whenever you can accumulate savings without the penalty of taxation — DO IT!

*Grateful thanks must be given for portions of this section to Mr. Dan F. Peternell, CLU, Regional Manager for Group and Pension for the Lincoln National Life Insurance Company, New Jersey Special Markets office in Clifton, New Jersey.

13 Objectives of Taxation

Stephen P. LaBarbera

W HAT BETTER way is there to develop an appreciation of taxation than by examining its objectives? The primary objective of federal and state taxation is to raise revenue. The funding required for the tremendous and ever growing federal and state government budgets is derived directly from the taxation process.

In addition to the revenue raising objective, it is generally believed that taxation policies are utilized to attain socially desirable goals. Congress achieves its social objectives by adding or amending sections of the Internal Revenue Code. An example of this would be the addition of Section 169 to the Code. This was incorporated in the Tax Reform Act of 1969, when the battle against pollution was one of the major social issues of the time. Section 169 was passed to induce industries to install pollution control facilities. This was accomplished by allowing industry to amortize certified pollution control facilities over a period of sixty months. This favorable amortization period encouraged many industries to install the facilities necessary to control air and water pollution.

The final objective of taxation is economic stabilization. Taxation can be used as a weapon to aid in the fight against inflation as well as a means to slow the growth of the economy. When the country is in a period of recession taxes are lowered reducing the burden on the people so they retain more of their earnings and increase their spending. This in turn stimulates the economy and creates more jobs. Raising taxes has the opposite effect and is utilized to slow the economy in periods of prosperity. The economy is quite complex and taxation is just one of the tools used to achieve economic stabilization.

TYPES OF TAXES

Most people are aware of federal income tax, state and city income tax, sales tax, property tax, and social security. All income taxes, whether federal, state, or city, are levied against income. Sales taxes, whether state or local, can be levied upon the retailer first or directly upon the consumer. Property taxes can be assessed against the owners of real or personal property. In 1980, both employer and employee must contribute to social security (FICA) at a rate of 6.65% each, against a taxable wage base of $29,700.

However, there are several other less familiar types of taxes that all of us may be paying. On the federal level additional existing taxes are: estate tax, gift tax, excise taxes, self-employment tax, import duties, passport fees, tax on telephone and teletype services, tax on air transportation of persons, truck use tax, and unemployment tax. The federal estate tax is levied after death against the deceased's estate. One of the objectives of estate planning is to avoid as much estate tax as possible, while disposing of the deceased's estate according to his instructions. All gifts in excess of $3000 per donee per year may be subject to the federal gift tax. The gift tax is assessable upon the donor and not the recipient (donee). Federal excise taxes are levied upon the sale of certain personal goods including: cigars, cigarettes, coal, distilled spirits, fermented liquor, firearms, fishing equipment, gasoline, lubricating oils, motor vehicles, tires and tubes, and wines. Self-employment tax is the equivalent of the wage earner's social security and is assessed on a self-employed individual's net earnings. The remaining federal taxes mentioned are levied on the sale of the items described.

On the state and local level there may also exist alcoholic beverage taxes, cigarette and tobacco taxes, automobile license and registration fees, unemployment taxes, gasoline taxes, gift tax, inheritance tax or estate tax, stamp taxes, and use taxes. The types of taxes levied vary from state to state.

Since many of these taxes are passed on to the consumer in the price of goods or services, it is difficult even to know when, or at what rate. It may be a good investment of your time and money to use the services of a tax expert or accountant to help you take advantage legally of the tax laws and regulations.

SELECTING A TAX PROFESSIONAL

An important consideration when filing your tax return is whether to prepare it yourself or seek the help of a tax professional. As a general rule, you are better off with a professional unless your gross income is under $20,000 and/or you qualify to file a short form (Federal Form 1040A).

If you belong to the group that would profit by utilizing a tax professional, how do you select the right one? Generally speaking, the most obvious place to look is usually a poor choice. The storefront tax preparers who emerge around tax time each year are often inexpensive. However, the old cliche "you get what you pay for" holds true. These preparers are often compensated by the number of returns generated and not by the time spent. Therefore, they are not about to get into the gray areas of tax law, where the biggest loopholes are found. The resulting return will reflect the lack of time spent on information gathering and consideration of all the possibilities.

Avoid the preparer who guarantees a refund or, even worse, asks you how large a refund you would like. The majority of these preparers do actually deliver a refund or the amount you request. However, if and when you are audited you will truly regret having hired such a devious preparer. For the most part the only way that he can produce a refund in the amount you specify is by fabricating various deductions. Unfortunately, that is fraud and by signing your return you are becoming a party to the fraud. Many people fall victim to this trap because getting a large refund each year is desirable. Sooner or later, however, you will end up regretting it.

There are three types of tax professionals worth considering when you are looking for qualified help: certified public accountants, tax attorneys, and enrolled agents. Locating a qualified specialist can be difficult. Your best sources for leads are your friends, colleagues, or possibly your legal advisor, insurance agent or local banker.

In your search you should shop around until you locate a professional who is credible to you. Feel free to discuss rates. These can vary from $20 to $100 or more per hour. You can even get an estimate by bringing along last year's return.

How much should the preparation of an average return cost? Let's assume you own your own home, your family gross income is in the $35,000 to $50,000 range, you have a few security transactions during the year, a couple of school-aged children and you claim your parents as dependents. The total cost would be between $150 to $300 and is tax deductible. In most cases a tax professional will save you more in taxes than he costs you in fees. You will also have peace of mind, knowing your tax return was properly prepared. If the IRS should call you in for an audit you have the option of going yourself or sending your preparer to represent you.

RECORDS AND DEDUCTIONS

Whether or not you hire a tax preparer, detailed records are always helpful. If you hire a professional, a good set of organized records saves the preparer time and lowers the fee. The reverse is also true. If you dump a shoe box full of unsorted receipts and cancelled checks on the preparer's desk, you will be paying a very high fee for some simple filing work.

It is often helpful to organize your documentation according to the major sections of the tax return. Your records consist of the schedules prepared by you and supported by receipts, cancelled checks, and any other form of written evidence available. Begin by collecting all documents pertaining to gross income. This includes: W-2 salary and wage statements; 1099 forms reporting savings account interest, dividend and interest from investments; brokerage statements and mutual fund statements establishing the amount of investment gains and losses; and all sources of miscellaneous income such as alimony, state and local tax refunds, pensions, annuities, rents, royalties, partnerships, estates or trusts, unemployment compensation, and any other income such as gambling winnings.

Next, collect all documentation for adjustments to income including: moving expense, employee business expenses, payments to an individual retirement account (IRA), payments to a Keogh retirement plan (H.R. 10), forfeited interest penalty for premature withdrawal of a Certificate of Deposit, etc., alimony paid, and disability income exclusion.

Organize your documentation for itemized deductions following the order on Schedule A — Itemized Deductions. Begin with medical and dental expenses including: health insurance payments, medical and dental costs not reimbursed by insurance, the cost of transportation for medical care, eyeglasses, hearing aids and dentures. The section for taxes includes state and local income taxes, real estate tax, sales tax, personal property tax. For sales tax deduction, keep track of your purchases carefully during the year. You can often come out ahead of the deduction you would get by using the sales tax tables, especially if your annual income is over $40,000. Interest payments on home mortgages, car and other installment loans, credit card accounts, and education loans are also deductible. Contributions should be separated into those for which you have receipts or cancelled checks and others which lack written evidence. Many people forget about casualty or theft losses from car accidents, storm or home vandalism. Finally, there are the miscellaneous deductions including union or professional dues, equipment, books or periodicals that pertain to your business, profession or investments, the cost of uniforms, support hose, and special shoes which are not used for normal wear, the cost of maintenance of uniforms during the year, safe deposit box expense, and last year's bill from your tax preparer.

Also consider whether you have any expenditures which qualify for tax credits. Tax credits are more beneficial than ordinary deductions because they are subtracted directly from your tax bill, while deductions only reduce the income on which you pay your taxes. The tax credit for political contributions was doubled beginning in the year 1979. If you made contributions to a candidate for public office, a political committee or to a newsletter fund of a candidate for public office, you can take a tax credit of one-half of your contribution but not more than $50 on a single return or $100 on a joint return. The tax credit can only be used for contributions to political campaigns intended to help a candidate get elected.

There are two kinds of residential energy credits available to the individual taxpayer, regardless of whether you own or rent your home. The only requirement is that the taxpayer actually pays for the qualifying items. Investments in renewable energy sources such as solar energy equipment, windpowered or geothermal energy equipment allows a credit equal to 30% of the first $2000 spent and 20% of the next $8000, for a maximum credit of $2200. There is also a credit for home energy conservation costs equal to 15% of the first $2000 spent on qualified items to save energy in a home built before

April 20, 1977. Items qualifying for this credit include: insulation, storm windows or doors, exterior caulking and weather stripping, automatic thermostats, fuel efficient furnace controls, and fuel efficient replacement burners. Both kinds of energy credits apply to items installed after April 19, 1977 and before January 1, 1986. In addition, new $10,000 and $2,000 limits apply for each new main residence during the effective period of the credit; after having fully used up your energy credit at your previous residence, you will in effect have a new credit available.

TAX PLANNING AND TAX SHELTERS

The objective of tax planning is to minimize the burden of taxation. Tax planning is a full-time activity. After January 1, your chances to make tax savings maneuvers for the previous year are gone.

Use your tax professional as a source of tax planning advice. Even if you choose not to use the services of a tax professional, there are still a number of potential tax savings techniques. As a general rule, take deductions as soon as possible, but defer income whenever possible until the following year. Everyone does not have control over their receipt of income but professionals may delay the billing of end-of-the-year clients, or employees may opt to receive their year-end bonuses in January. This will not only save you tax in the current year but will also delay the payment of tax until the following year.

If, during the year, you have realized any capital gains from the sale for profit of stock, land, jewelry or any other capital asset, review your other assets to see if you have had any offsetting losses. This will save you tax and also relieve you of investments that are not keeping up with inflation. When dealing with capital assets, always strive to have short-term losses (capital asset held one year or less) and long term gains (capital asset held more than one year). Short-term capital losses are particularly valuable, since they can offset up to $3000 of ordinary income on a dollar-for-dollar basis. Long-term capital losses require two dollars of loss to offset one dollar of ordinary income. Long-term capital gains are valuable because net long-term gains are 60% tax-free. In other words, only 40% of your net long-term capital gains is added to ordinary income, while net short-term capital gains are fully included in ordinary income.

If you have an asset that has substantially appreciated (increased in value) consider selling it on an installment basis, receiving the proceeds over a period of more than one year. This spreads out your gain over the period in which you receive the proceeds. Thus, you are benefitted by delaying the payment of a portion of the taxes due, as well as saving taxes by spreading out your gain over a number of years.

Be sure to pay all allowable tax deduction items before the year is out. One exception to that rule is medical expenses. A taxpayer is entitled to a deduction for medical expenses paid during the year in excess of 3% of adjusted gross income. If the medical expense comes near the end of the year, the taxpayer may save tax money by carefully choosing the year in which to pay the bill. For example, a person with adjusted gross income of $20,000 must have paid medical expenses in excess of $600 to get a medical expense deduction. If he has a doctor bill in December for $400, and only $100 of additional medical expenses during the year, it would be better to wait to pay the bill until the next year, when a total of more than $600 may be reached. However, if he had additional medical expenses over the $600 limitation then it would be beneficial to pay the December bill before the end of the year.

For people who pay quarterly estimated state income taxes, the last payment is due in January. State and local taxes are deductible on your return in the year you pay them. You can prepay your last installment in December and take a deduction in that year. Likewise, if you are planning the purchase of a car or boat you can deduct the sales tax if you buy it before the year is out.

Persons who are self-employed can set up a Keogh plan (H.R. 10) which provides for retirement income and a current deduction from income equal to 15% of earned income or $7500, whichever is less. A person who is not self-employed but earns money moonlighting can also pay in a portion of his free-lance income. You can deduct contributions made to an existing Keogh plan as late as April 15 on your previous year's tax return. However new Keogh plans must be set up before year end if you wish to qualify for deductions on your previous year's tax return.

As explained in chapter 12, individual retirement accounts (IRA) are similar to Keoghs but are for employees who are not active participants in qualified plans at their companies or in governmental plans. Cash paid by or on behalf of an individual to his individual retirement account can be deducted. The deduction is equal to the lesser of $1500 or 15% of compensation on earned income. A taxpayer may set up and add to an IRA as late as April 15 and still qualify for a deduction on his previous year's return.

These are examples of some of the basic tax planning techniques which are available to the ordinary taxpayer. The larger and more complicated your tax picture, the more exotic are the tax planning tools available. One of these more complicated tax savings and deferral devices is the tax shelter. Today, tax shelters are currently marketed as "tax advantaged" or "tax incentive" investments. In 1978 major brokerage houses sold an estimated 1.8 billion dollars' worth of tax shelters, more than double the sales for the previous year. The demand for tax shelters has been increasing because more and more people have been pushed into top tax brackets by inflation.

According to experts, taxpayers are candidates to invest in tax shelters once they hit the 49% federal tax bracket. For a married couple in 1979 that was achieved when their taxable income reached $45,800 and for a single individual the amount was $34,100.

Two of the more popular shelters for the small investors who are seeking tax relief are real estate or oil and gas ventures. These shelters are sold through brokers, lawyers and accountants. They usually take the form of a limited partnership. Individual investors (the limited partners) supply the bulk of the financing while the general partner or sponsor runs the business aspects of the shelter, for example, constructing the building, or drilling the well.

The basic purpose of all tax shelters is to provide investors current deductions while creating capital gains when the shelter is terminated. The income deductions allow the investor to reduce his income, while the favorable capital gains treatment allows the investor to receive 60% of his final profit tax free.

Despite their attractions, shelters have many pitfalls. They are intrinsically risky: in an exploratory oil shelter the driller may find dust. If the IRS suspects that a tax shelter is merely a facade, it can disallow deductions, or surprise investors with higher than expected taxes on gains. Each year, there are many tax shelters sold that are not properly financed or are very questionable. One way to protect yourself is to invest with public partnerships — those that are required to be registered with the Securities and Exchange Commission (S.E.C.) — as opposed to private placements.

If you are considering investment in a tax shelter you should investigate the sales representative's firm to be sure they are reputable and possess a successful track record.

HOW TO PREPARE FOR AND HANDLE
AN AUDIT BY THE IRS

Anticipated audits by the IRS often cause panic and worry. Knowing how to prepare yourself and how to handle the upcoming audit can relieve your anxiety and save you money.

Each year, the Treasury Department publishes a chart of Average Itemized Deductions by income classes, and the most recent figures available, for the year 1977, are reproduced below:

Table 13-1. Average Itemized Deductions for 1977 by Adjusted Gross Income Classes:

Adjusted Gross Income Classes	Average Deductions for Contributions	Average Deductions for Interest	Average Deductions for Taxes	Average Medical, Dental Deductions	Total Deductions as % of AGI
$ 4,000—$ 6,000	$426	$1,370	$ 932	$1,693	72%
6,000— 8,000	513	1,607	1,052	1,368	57%
8,000— 10,000	524	1,507	1,147	1,100	44%
10,000— 12,000	527	1,589	1,179	882	38%
12,000— 14,000	475	1,706	1,242	806	33%
14,000— 16,000	479	1,868	1,421	669	30%
16,000— 18,000	559	1,880	1,553	670	28%
18,000— 20,000	532	2,006	1,720	596	26%
20,000— 25,000	563	2,085	1,954	505	23%
25,000— 30,000	676	2,271	2,300	520	21%
30,000— 50,000	893	2,637	3,124	551	20%
50,000—100,000	1,965	4,230	5,488	748	19%
100,000 or more	9,673	9,345	13,839	1,063	19%

This chart should not be considered as indicating amounts which would be allowed by the IRS, but only as guidelines. You should also know that if your deductions are above the averages for your income bracket, it does not necessarily mean that your return will be selected for audit. If your deductions are well below the averages, this may indicate that you are spending less than other taxpayers in your bracket, or that your personal expenditures may not be tax deductible. For example, a taxpayer who pays rent gets no deduction for rent expense while the houseowner may deduct the interest charges on his home mortgage as well as property taxes paid. Finally, there is the possibility that you are overlooking some deductions. In any case, these averages do not automatically entitle you to deduct the average amount for your income bracket. You must always be able to substantiate all claimed deductions on your return.

When your return is received by the IRS, it is key punched and fed into a computer which tests for mathematical errors and items which clearly are not allowed. If an error is found, a correction notice is sent to you with a request for payment if your tax is understated, or a refund check if your tax is overstated. Just because a refund is received it does not mean that your return will not be audited. As a general rule the IRS has three years from the due date of the return to call you in for an examination.

The majority of returns selected for audit are selected by a computer which is programmed with a complex set of standards scoring various items on a return. A return receiving a high score suggests a strong probability of error and qualifies the return for audit. The computer's selection is then reviewed by agents, who decide whether your return should be selected for an examination. Returns may also be selected on a totally random basis. Each year returns are selected at random and the information gathered from these examinations is used by the IRS to update and improve its computer program for scoring future returns.

If your return is selected for examination, you will be notified by a letter which will inform you of the place and method of examination. Some audits are handled exclusively by correspondence. When only a specific item or two is questioned the IRS may request substantiation in the form of a photocopy by return mail. Other more detailed audits will require either you or your appointed representative to appear in an IRS office for review of your records by an office auditor. If your return is supported by voluminous records your return will usually be assigned (or you may request that it be assigned) to a revenue agent who will conduct a field audit in your home or place of business.

The first decision you must make is whether or not you want to represent yourself before the IRS or hire a professional to accompany or represent you on the audit. If you had someone else prepare your return, ask for advice as to whether he should represent you or whether you can do just as well without him. An attorney, a certified public accountant, an individual enrolled to practice before the IRS, or the person who prepared your return and signed it as the preparer, may represent or accompany you.

If you prepare your return and it is complicated, you may be better off hiring a professional to represent you. There are several reasons for this: IRS agents prefer to deal with a professional who speaks the same language; a professional has more experience dealing with IRS agents and may even have had previous contacts with the agent assigned to your audit; and finally a professional will not get as emotionally involved with the audit of your return and thus can remain more objective in his negotiations with the IRS representative.

If you should decide to represent yourself before the IRS your basic plan should be to finish the audit as quickly as possible and to complete the audit with the least possible assessment of additional tax. To accomplish these goals, it is of paramount importance that you are thoroughly prepared. Spend as much time as possible reviewing your return and accumulating substantiation such as receipts and cancelled checks.

Be aware that an agent possesses a considerable amount of discretion when conducting an examination. There are many areas in which he can rule either way. If you are well prepared and impress the agent that you are basically honest, he will be much more reasonable and will usually make concessions where an occasional item cannot be located.

Another helpful hint relates to your appearance. A person who attends an audit dressed in an expensive suit or wearing furs and plenty of diamonds can arouse an agent's attention. As a general rule, try to underdress for the occasion.

Finally — and most important — refrain from volunteering any information. Many people get themselves into trouble simply by talking too much. Basically, you should let the agent set the pace of the examination. Listen carefully to any questions you are asked and answer them as specifically and honestly as possible. Taxpayers have been known to have informed agents of improper deductions on their returns as a result of their having misinterpreted an agent's question.

If you were not honest when filling out your return, don't admit to an IRS representative that you deliberately intended to defraud the government. When you are caught with a faked deduction or undeclared income, the facts will speak for themselves. Don't make things worse by confessing. Any reasonable excuse will usually satisfy the agent unless your transgression is such that it can't conceivably be ascribed to anything but willful fraud. In a fraud action the government has the difficult burden of proof. The government must demonstrate that your act of fraud was deliberate. By confessing, you are making their case much easier to prove. In all likelihood, the agent would also prefer not to make a fraud case out of it. He would rather be in the field working on a new audit than sitting in a courtroom. If a fraud case should be declared against you, consult a lawyer.

Upon completion of the audit, you will be asked to sign an agreement form. By signing, you indicate your agreement to the findings and the adjusted amounts on the form. If you do not agree with the findings of the examiner, and the examination was made either in an IRS office or by correspondence, you may request an immediate meeting with a supervisor to explain your position. If you do not agree with the supervisor or with a revenue agent in a field audit case, you will be sent a copy of the examination report explaining the proposed adjustments and a transmittal letter detailing the appeals available to you. You have thirty days to inform the IRS of your intended actions. At this point, depending on the amounts of additional tax due, your best bet will be to seek professional advice regarding any further negotiations or appeals.

As Samuel Pepys said in his diary, "It gives me some kind of content to remember how painful it is sometimes to keep money, as well as to get it."

References

1. Aguilera, Donna and Messick, Janice M. *Crisis Intervention* (2nd ed.). St. Louis: Mosby, 1974.

2. Altfest, Lewis J. and Lichner, Alan B. *Introduction to Business.* New York: Barnes and Noble, 1978.

3. *Am. J. Nurs.* January 1981. How can I get a job on Capitol Hill?

4. Bistline, Susan and Philos, Daphne. What every trainer should know about copyright. *Training/HRD.* November, 1976.

5. Bolles, Richard Nelson. *What Color Is Your Parachute?* (1980 ed.). Berkeley: Ten Speed Press, 1980.

6. Bornstein, Julie. A legal overview. In Margo C. Neal (ed.). *Nurses in Business: An Alternative.* Pacific Palisades, Ca.: Nurseco, (in press).

7. Buskirk, Richard H. and Miles, Beverly. *Beating Men at Their Own Game.* New York: Wiley, 1980.

8. Charlton, James (Ed.). *The Writer's Quotation Book: A Literary Companion.* Yonkers: Pushcart Press, 1980.

9. Ellis, Janice R. and Hartley, Celia L. The world of employment. *Nursing in Today's World* P. 146, 1980

10. Godfrey, Marjorie A. Job satisfaction—or should that be dissatisfaction? How nurses feel about nursing, part two. *Nursing in Today's World.* P. 18, May, 1978.

11. Gordon, Arleen. Marketing CE: the bottom line. In Signe S. Cooper and Margo C. Neal (ed.). *Perspectives on Continuing Education in Nursing.* Pacific Palisades, Ca.: Nurseco, 1981.

12. Juliette, Ronald A. Copyright: knowing the basics. *National Society for Performance and Instruction Journal.* March, 1981.

13. King, David and Levine, Karen. *The Best Way in the World for a Woman to Make Money.* New York: Warner Books, 1979.

14. Morris, Kay and Trygstad, Jim. *Entry Into Practice—A Career Entry Guide for Nurses.* Nashville, Tn: Manpower Data Corp., in press.

15. Neal, Margo C. The independent provider: an innovative role. In Signe S. Cooper and Margo C. Neal. (Eds.). *Perspectives on Continuing Education in Nursing.* Pacific Palisades, Ca.: Nurseco, 1981.

16. Nursing 80 Career Directory, Finding your niche. Intermed Publications. Pp. 22–23 January, 1980.

17. Pile, Stephan. *The Incomplete Book of Failures.* New York: Dutton, 1979.

18. Rowland, Howard S. Manpower and jobs for nurses. *The Nurse's Almanac* 71:68, 1978.

Suggestions for Further Reading

Ahern, Dee Dee with Bliss, Betsy. *The Economics of Being a Woman.* New York: McGraw-Hill, 1977.

Baccalaureate education in nursing: key to a professional career in nursing. New York: National League for Nursing, 1978.

Bender, James F. *How to Sell Well.* New York: McGraw-Hill, 1971.

Brownstone, David M., Franek, Irene M., and Carruth, Gorton. *The V.N.R. Dictionary of Business and Finance.* New York: Van Nostrand Reinhold, 1980.

Clay, William C., Jr. *Estate Planning.* Homewood, Ill.: Irwin, 1977.

Crispen, Margaret. *How Any Woman Can Get Rich Fast in Real Estate.* New York: Warner Books, 1978.

Donovan, Lynn. Can you really make more as a grocery clerk? *R.N.,* March, 1980.

Epstein, R. B., and Friesner, A. Caution! this baccalaureate may be hazardous to your health. *A.J.N.* P. 470, March, 1970.

Esper, Rosemary O. Getting a new job. *A.J.N.* April, 1981.

Hyatt, Carole. *The Woman's Selling Game.* New York: Warner Books, 1979.

Jackson, Stephanie. What do consultants do, anyway? *National Society for Performance and Instruction Journal.* November, 1979.

Lenburg, Carrie B. In search of the BSN: how to decide which program does you justice. *R.N.* February, 1980.

Lucas, Andrea L. What's nursing worth? *R.N.* January, 1980.

McGrath, B. Baccalaureate nursing education for the RN: why is it so scarce? *J. Nurs. Ed.* P. 40, June, 1979.

Murray, Neil. Job-hunting credo: contacts. *American Way.* July, 1980.

Nicoll, Joyce. A nurse-owned rural health clinic. *Nurse Practitioner.* November–December, 1979.

Porter, Sylvia. *New Money Book for the 80's.* New York: Avon Books, 1980.

Reed, F. C. Education or exploitation. *A.J.N.* 1095, June, 1979.

Robinson, Alice M. and Notter, Lucille E. *Clinical Writing for Health Professionals.* Baltimore, Md., 1981.

Rogers, Mary and Joyce, Nancy. *Women and Money.* New York: Avon Books, 1979.

Sherwood, Hugh C. *How to Invest in Bonds.* New York: McGraw-Hill, 1976.

Slainka, S. C. Finding funds for further education. *Nursing '79,* June, 1979.

Taylor, John R. *How to Start and Succeed in a Business of Your Own.* Reston, Va.: Reston Publishing Co., 1978.

Thomas, Lewis. Notes on punctuation. *The Medusa and the Snail.* New York: Penguin, 1979.

Training/HRD. Mentors seen as key allies in career growth. August, 1980.

Wiley, Loy Are you promotable? *Nursing '80.* July, 1980.

Wilson, Aubrey. *The Marketing of Professional Services.* New York: Newsweek Books, 1979.

Winston, Sandra. *The Entrepreneurial Woman.* New York: Newsweek Books, 1979.

Young, Katherine Jean, RN. Independent Nurse Practitioner: The Practical Issues of Practice (an interview with M. Lucille Kinlein, RN). *Nurse Practitioner.* Jan-Feb. 1977: 14–17 (vol. 2, no. 1).

Glossary

Accidental death benefit — an addition to a life insurance policy for payment of a further benefit in case of death as a result of accidental means (often called "Double Indemnity").

Advance — the amount of money a corporation gives a sales representative. This is considered guaranteed income. It is based upon the stipulation that when you sell enough of your product to equal your advance you earn commission above the advance. In publishing, an advance is a loan against future royalties.

Amortization — the reduction and ultimate full payment of a mortgage debt over a specified period of time through installment payments that include both interest and principal.

Annual report — a report of a corporation's yearly operating expenses, its year-end financial condition, a balance sheet, operating statement, auditor's report and management comments.

Annuity — a contract that provides an income for a specific period of time, either for a number of years or for a person's lifetime.

Appraisal — an estimate of the value of a parcel of real estate or other asset, denoting its probable sale price.

Appreciation — increase in value, usually related to various economic causes such as inflation.

Appurtenances — whatever may be attached to land that will accompany it at time of sale, such as garage, poolhouse, etc.

Assessment — tax placed on property to pay for an improvement by an authority.

Asset — anything of value that is owned and that can be converted into cash.

Assignment — transfer of a lease, contract, title, etc., to some other party.

"Bear" market — when the overall price decline is substantial and prolonged (a down market).

Beneficiary — the person (or trust fund) named in an insurance policy to whom the benefit is to be paid upon the death of the insured.

Bid and asked — the "bid" price for a stock is the highest price that anyone has declared he is willing to pay for a share of stock at a given time. The "asked" price is the lowest price at which anyone has declared he is willing to sell his share at a given time.

Binder — an agreement in advance to purchase property, usually involving a deposit.

Bond — an interest-bearing debt instrument issued by a government or a company, which promises to pay specific sums at certain intervals, with interest paid in installments and principal paid in one lump sum.

Book value — a corporation's total assets less its liabilities and the liquidating value of its preferred stock divided by the number of shares of common stock outstanding. Used to determine the figure on a per-share basis.

Broker (insurance) — an individual licensed by the state to sell insurance but not representing or limited to one company. Other brokers include stock, real estate, money and mortgage specialists.

Brokerage fees — fees to brokers for transactions arranged between buyers and sellers.

Budget — a formal estimate of future income and expenses.

"Bull market" — when the overall price rise of stocks is substantial and prolonged (an up market).

Call — when the corporation exercises its right to redeem a bond in advance of its maturity date.

Capital gains — the profits realized from a sale of securities, real estate or other capital assets.

Carrying charges — fees stemming from asset ownership such as interest on margin accounts, for warehousing goods, or retaining possession of purchased property.

Cash surrender value (cash value) — the amount available in cash upon surrender of an insurance policy before it becomes payable by death or maturity.

C.D.'s — see *certificate of deposit.*

Certificate of deposit — a receipt for a bank deposit in certificate instead of passbook form that bears interest and is payable after a specified amount of time.

Chattels — personal property such as fixtures, furnishings and household goods.

Closed end funds — shares offered to the public that must be bought and sold in the over-the-counter market.

Closing costs — charges paid at the time of closing and property transfer, usually by the buyer, including costs for attorney's fees, title search, title insurance and property survey.

Codicil — an addition to a will that modifies the will and its conditions.

Collateral — real or personal property used as security for a loan. The collateral can become the property of the lender upon default on the loan.

Co-maker — a non-recipient of a loan who signs a debt document making him responsible for repayment of the loan.

Commission (real estate) — fee paid to a realtor, usually by the seller, for locating a buyer. It is a fixed percentage of the selling price.

Commodity futures — contracts between buyers and sellers stating the prices, terms and delivery of commodities at a future time.

Common stock — a standard form of shared ownership in a corporation.

Compound interest — a system of computing interest by adding simple interest to the original sum and then using the resulting amount as a basis for computing subsequent interest.

Condominium — a building or series of buildings in which each buyer owns his own unit and an interest in the common areas of the development.

Conservator — a person appointed by a court to guard and protect the property of a person found to be incompetent to manage his own interests.

Consideration — the payments (or one of regular periodical payments) a policyowner must make for an annuity or a retirement annuity.

Consumption cost — the price paid for goods or services that are used up, e.g., rent.

Contributory pension plan — a jointly financed pension plan consisting of contributions from the employees and the employer.

Conversion premium — the difference between a bond's market price and its conversion value.

Conversion ratio — the right to convert a bond into a specified number of shares of the issuing company's preferred or common stock.

Conversion value — the value of the shares into which a bond may be converted.

Convertible bond — see *conversion ratio*.

Convertible term insurance — term insurance providing the right of exchange for a permanent plan of insurance.

Cooperative — a form of apartment living in which a buyer obtains shares in a corporation that owns the building and holds its mortgage.

Corporation — a business that legally functions as an individual under law and is regarded as an individual in the eyes of the law.

Corporate bond — see *bond*.

Credit union — an organization that lends money to members at lower interest rates than those of commercial lenders out of funds deposited by the membership.

Co-signer — see *co-maker*.

Debentures — the issuance of bonds without the backing of collateral. Debentures are only as good as the issuer's ability to meet debt obligations.

Decedent's estate — everything owned by a person at his death including both real and personal property. Essentially the sum of a person's accumulated wealth upon his death.

Deed — a legal document conveying title to real estate.

Default — the inability of the issuer of a bond to pay principle, interest or both to bondholders.

Depletion allowance — the value reductions set for depletion of specified natural resources.

Depreciation — loss in value of buildings over a period of time. Tax laws permit an allowance for depreciation against a property's net receipts, thereby reducing the owner's taxable income.

Depression — a long-term economic crisis, with widespread unemployment and the collapse of major economic institutions.

Discount bond — a bond that sells at less than its face value. An older bond that pays a very low rate of interest.

Discretionary bonus — a nonspecific bonus determined by management based on perceptions of the effort and/or results of a salesperson's activity.

Discretionary income — money that is not committed to pay for basic life sustaining necessities and can be used for entertainment or investment.

Dividend (insurance) — a return of part of the premium on limited types of insurance.

Dividend (stocks) — a part of the earnings or profit made by a company that is paid to stockholders.

Double indemnity — see *Accidental death benefit.*

Dow Jones Averages — an average composed of thirty well known industrial, transportation and utility common stock values. Widely quoted as indicating the general rise or fall of stock market prices.

Easement rights — rights of use of lands owned by another, such as access road, shared driveway, etc., water company, electric company and sewer lines often have easements over or across neighboring properties.

Eminent domain — government rights to acquire private property for public use without owner's consent, provided reasonable compensation is made.

Endowment insurance — an insurance plan providing a defined sum to the policyowner (or beneficiary) after a specified number of years.

Enrolled agent — a professional tax preparer who has passed a special examination that is administered by the treasury department.

Entrepreneur — a person who develops a business enterprise and takes complete responsibility for its management.

Equity — investment of capital with reasonable assurance of increase in the value of the dollars invested.

ERISA (Employee Retirement Income Security Act) — government legislation (1974) providing specific requirements on vesting of pension benefits to employees by employer contributions.

Escrow — money or documents held by a third party pending fulfillment of the conditions of a contract.

Exclusive listing — a property listed for sale with only one real estate broker who has rights to sell it in a specified time period.

Executor — an individual appointed by a maker of a will to carry out

the provisions of the will and the wishes of the maker, after
death.

Face amount — the dollar amount stated on the face of an insurance
policy to be paid in case of death or at maturity.

Face value — see *Face amount.*

Family policy — a life insurance contract providing coverage for several family members. Can be a combination of whole life
and term on the individuals insured, as well as those born
after the policy is issued.

F.D.I.C. (Federal Deposit Insurance Corp.) — an independent federal
agency that insures deposits up to a certain limit in national
and state banks that are part of the Federal Reserve System
or have applied for such insurance.

Federal National Mortgage Association ("Fannie Mae") — a private corporation under government charter that provides a market for
mortgages held by banks and savings and loan associations,
i.e., the secondary mortgage market.

Federal Reserve Bank — one of twelve central Federal Banks in the
United States operating in twelve respective Federal Reserve
Districts.

Fiduciary — one holding a position of trust with legal status as a
trustee to execute or administer an estate.

Financial statement — a statement indicating the current financial position of an individual or a corporation that may include a
balance sheet, profit and loss statement or flow of funds
statement.

Foreclosure — a legal process forcing the sale of your property when
there is default on payments.

Fringe benefits — employee compensation beyond wages and salaries.
May include insurance, pensions, profit-sharing, sick leave,
tuition assistance and vacations.

Government bond — a bond issued by the government or an agency of
the government.

Grace period — time duration (usually thirty-one days) following
premium due dates, during which an overdue premium may
be paid.

Growth stock — common stock that has appreciated in value quickly,
reflecting an excellent future for the issuing corporation.

Hedging — the use of alternative courses of action in order to minimize risk.

Homeowner's insurance — property insurance covering hazards such as
fire, weather, theft or personal liabilities.

"HR-10" — see *Keogh Plan.*

Incentive bonus — any form of bonus or commission, as opposed to guaranteed salary, used to motivate people to increase productivity or to reward performance.

Income averaging — the ability to lump current income and several previous year's income for figuring federal personal income tax rates.

Income property — real estate property that is used by its owner primarily as a source of income.

Individual Retirement Account (IRA) — under Federal law an arrangement available to individuals not covered by a company retirement plan, for a tax-advantaged pension plan.

Inflation — a general increase in the level of prices within the economy, accompanied by a decrease in the purchasing power of money used in that economy.

Inheritance — personal wealth or property that is received through a bequest from another person.

I.R.A. — see *Individual Retirement Account.*

Inter vivos — a legal term applicable to the transfer of property from one living person to another via a trust or gift.

Insurance — a fund, generally administered by a corporation or governmental body which guarantees or indemnities the insured against specific losses.

Investment banker — a banker who agrees to buy an issuer's bonds and resell them to the public.

Investment club — a group of people who meet regularly, formalizing rules and defining investment goals, to invest and share in any profits on their investments.

Investment cost — the price paid for goods or services that add additional value or increase the capital spent.

Joint ownership — two or more persons holding equal ownership of property with the right to become sole owner if they remain the sole survivor.

Joint tenancy — see *Joint ownership.*

Keogh Plan — a government retirement plan for self-employed persons and/or partners to build a tax-deferred retirement fund.

Key money — a payment sometimes requested by brokers, made to obtain a dwelling unit in areas where apartments are scarce (within the law, although somewhat frowned upon).

Lapsed policy — a policy terminated at the end of the grace period for non-payment of premium.

Lead — a prospective customer who has expressed interest in your product.

Leveraging — investing with borrowed money.

Liability coverage — a form of insurance protecting a policy holder from claims regarding any type of negligence on his part.

Life annuity — a contract providing an income for life.

Limited partnership — investment in a tax-shelter, project or business headed by a general partner who manages the operation and receives a fee.

Liquid assets — cash, marketable securities, and notes less an allowance for collectibles.

Living trust — see *Inter vivos.*

Load — the levying of sales charges on initial purchases of mutual funds.

Loan value (insurance) — the amount that can be borrowed (at a specific interest rate) under an insurance policy by the policyowner, using the policy itself as collateral.

Margin — a requirement of the Federal Reserve System that an investor put up at least fifty percent of the value when purchasing stocks.

Margin account — an account with a brokerage firm in which credit is extended to customers for the purchase of securities within the guidelines of the Securities and Exchange Commission.

Marketing — activities undertaken to advertise, promote, sell and deliver products or services.

Money–Market funds — short-term investments that often mature in no more than one year. Funds usually invested in U.S. Government or agency securities, bank certificates of deposit, banker's acceptances and commercial paper.

Mortgage — a conditional transfer of real property as security for the payment of a debt.

Mortgagee — the person, bank or savings institution to whom the property is mortgaged.

Mortgage insurance — insures private lenders against losses stemming from mortgage and housing loans and is a federally funded program.

Mortgagor — an owner who conveys his property as security for a loan (the borrower or debtor).

Multiple listing — a property listed for sale with one real estate broker and shared with fellow brokers, with commission divided at time of sale between listing broker, selling broker and multiple listing board.

Mutual fund — an investment fund that invests on behalf of individuals in money market funds, bonds or stocks.

Mutual Life Insurance Company — a life insurance company owned by its policyholders that returns dividends on surplus earnings.

Negotiations — the process of bargaining between contracting parties to satisfy agreements.

No load fund — a mutual fund that does not levy charges on its investors such as sales or management fees.

Non-liquid asset — one not easily converted to cash.

Non-participating insurance — a type of insurance on which no dividends are paid.

Odd-lot — an amount of stock normally less than 100 shares.

Open listing — an oral or general listing.

Option (call) — a request to buy an option.

Option (put) — a request to place an order to sell.

Option (real estate) — the right to lease or purchase a property at a certain price within a designated time period.

Over-the-counter market — a market for stocks or bonds that are traded directly between buyers through a dealer and are not listed on any stock exchange.

Partnership — the commitment and association of two or more individuals, accepting unlimited liability, for the purpose of conducting a business for profit.

P/E — see *Price earnings ratio.*

Performance bonus — a monetary reward determined by sales management based on attainment of quotas.

Pension — financial resources set aside during one's employment and paid as income after retirement or leaving a company, in a series of payments for the balance of his lifetime.

Plan administrator — company employee handling its retirement plan.

Points — fees for setting up a loan or mortgage.

Preferred stock — a type of ownership that confers equity in a company. Preferred stockholders receive dividends and sometimes share in profits beyond specified dividends before common stockholders.

Premium — one of the regular payments a policyowner must make for an insurance policy.

Price-earnings ratio — the relationship between the current market price of a stock and its yearly earnings per share.

Prime rate — the rate of interest that banks charge corporate customers of the highest quality.

Principal — an amount of money invested on which a return in profit or interest may accrue over a period of time.

Probate — the court's validation of a will.

Profit sharing — an additional compensation, usually in the form of stock, options or cash, paid by a corporation to its employees for performance or upon retiring.

Proprietor — any owner of a business.

Prospectus — a detailed description of all financial data of a corporation offering stock for sale, to help potential investors evaluate the securities.

Proxy — official authorization given to a corporate representative to vote shares at a shareholder's meeting.

Quote — see *bid and asked.*

Real estate — land or real property as distinguished from personal property.

Realtor — an active member of a local real estate board affiliated with the National Association of Real Estate Boards.

Refinancing — an extension of the time of repayment of a debt by replacement with new debt. Done for the convenience or economic necessity of the borrower.

Remortgaging — see *refinancing.*

Reverse mortgage — a method of financing that allows a person who owns a debt-free home to borrow money against the equity of the home. Less costly than remortgaging.

Rider — an addition to a policy that restricts or expands its coverage.

Rollover — replacement of an existing debt with a new debt.

Savings and Loan Association — a savings bank specializing in home mortgage loans.

Securities and Exchange Commission (S.E.C.) — an investigative and regulatory federal agency that registers and regulates securities traded and firms engaged in trading.

Semi-detached house — one building containing two residences and separated by a common wall (often called a "duplex").

Sinking fund — a method by which a company raises capital by setting aside a fixed number of dollars each year.

Small Business Administration (S.B.A.) — an agency of the Federal government responsible for the administration of loans and information to stimulate growth of small businesses.

Speculation — high risk purchases of volatile common stock or property in hope of quick or high profits.

Spread — the difference between what a dealer pays for a bond (bid price) and what he is willing to sell it for (asked price).

Standard and Poor's Index — an index maintained by the Standard and Poor Corporation of 500 stocks, mainly industrial, rail and utilities, based on price movements and considered a representative indicator of the entire stock market.

Stock — a negotiable instrument indicating an ownership share in a public or privately held corporation.

Stock split — a corporate vote that initiates action to increase the number of shares by dividing the current outstanding shares.

Straight commission — a percentage of gross sales paid to a salesperson that does not guarantee a fixed amount of income.

Survey — an exact measurement of an owner's property.

Tax shelter — an investment vehicle that permits an individual in a relatively high tax bracket to make an investment in an entity whose form and proposed operations will provide special income tax savings.

Term insurance — a plan providing protection for only a limited period of time.

Title (deed) — proof that one is the legal owner of a property.

Title insurance — an insurance policy guaranteeing against the loss of a property in case of any defects in the title.

Traders — wholesalers and distributors who buy and sell goods, services and instruments of value.

Trust deed — see *mortgage*.

Truth in Lending Law — a federal law which states that every lending institution charging interest or finance charges must inform borrowers of the annual interest rate.

Unit trust — a fund that consists of corporate or municipal bonds. No fund management is provided beyond the initial selection of the bonds.

Variable annuity — an annuity contract wherein the amount of each payment fluctuates according to the cost of living index, security market values and other variable factors.

Variance — an allowance for a change in zoning requirements.

Vesting — the process whereby monies accumulated for an individual's retirement through a company plan cannot be taken away from him after a specified period of time.

Waiver — the surrender of a right, privilege or claim.

Waiver of premium — a provision (used most often in total disability benefits) keeping the policy in force without the payment of premiums.

Warrant — a privilege to buy a security at a specified price, within a specified period of time or perpetually.

Whole life insurance (straight life) — a plan providing protection for as long as the insured person lives, requiring premium payments for the same period.

Yield — yearly dividend value divided by the cost of the stock.

Yield (current) — reflects the relationship between the price a bond sells at in the open market and its interest rate.

Yield (to maturity) — reflects the interest on a bond, plus any profit or loss that will accrue when the bond matures.